Decorative
FABRIC
PAINTING

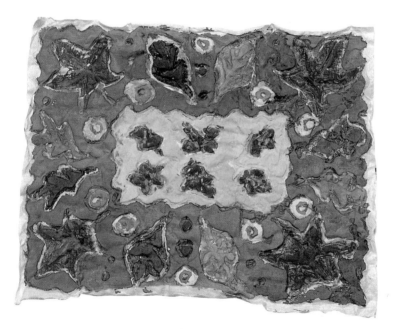

Decorative
FABRIC
PAINTING

ROSI ROBINSON

MEREHURST

For Louis, Laurie and Georgie

Published in 1994 by Merehurst Limited, Ferry House
51–57 Lacy Road, Putney, London SW15 1PR

ISBN 1 85391 293 X

A catalogue record of this book is available from
the British Library.

Edited by **Heather Dewhurst**
Designed by **Maggie Aldred**
Photography by **Jon Bouchier**

Typeset by J&L Composition Ltd, Filey, North Yorkshire
Colour separation by Global Colour, Malaysia
Printed in Italy by Amilcare Pizzi SpA

Contents

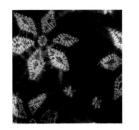

Introduction

What on earth am I doing writing a book about fabric painting? After all, I graduated from Vassar College, New York, with a history degree. But art is like life. Luck plays a big part. A Postgraduate Teaching Certificate course at Redland College, Bristol, included an introduction to fabric printing and batik. I was hooked.

Twenty-five years later, Mary Dowling, the teacher who helped me take my first faltering steps rang to tell me she had seen one of my pictures hanging in a friend's house. She was thrilled that a chance encounter with batik had been so important to me. (Mary Dowling herself has since transferred her talents to stained glass. Shame!)

So there it is. Instead of history, I ended up teaching art, printing and dyeing. Through the years, I have taught all ages from the uninhibited sevens to the meticulous seventies. For the last seven years I have been Head of Art at Cumnor House School in Sussex. As part of the National Curriculum I cover all types of painting, printing and dyeing on fabric and paper. Though many of my pupils have had success winning art scholarships and prizes in national competitions, like the prestigious Cadbury National Children's Art Competition, the biggest thrill is to introduce them to fabric and dye and watch them discover their own creativity; to see them proudly wear some colourful garments they have made themselves; and to see their pictures framed and mounted and given pride of place in their parents' living room. I hope that is what *Decorative Fabric Painting* will do for you.

Designing and printing your own cushion covers, curtains or tablecloths may sound like a daunting task, but in fact it can be highly creative. It is quicker, cheaper, and certainly more rewarding to create your own fabric pieces for the house. It can reflect your personality much better and give your home a unique character. This book demonstrates various techniques of fabric painting, with projects which you can follow for each technique. Once you understand the basic methods, you will be able to adapt them to whatever project you find most suitable.

I have divided the book into four sections. The first section describes the materials you will use. It gives a brief description of how to set about planning a design, the type of fabrics most suitable and the various dyes or fabric paints that can be applied.

The second section concentrates on painting and printing techniques used for surface design. Once you have had fun experimenting, I'm sure you will have the confidence to try some of the projects.

The third section concentrates on techniques of resist dyeing. Here, instead of simply painting the colours onto the surface of the fabric, the dye colour is impregnated into the fibres – the areas that are tied or painted with wax or gutta resist the colour.

The final section of the book is devoted to a

list of reliable suppliers you can approach for fabric painting materials, and an index.

SEARCHING FOR INSPIRATION

You cannot expect inspiration to strike just like that. However, you can prepare yourself by keeping a record of appealing images that will stimulate you when you sit down to start work. Teach yourself to look around you. Collect ideas – keep a scrapbook with sketches, pictures from magazines, colour schemes, shapes and textures. Take photographs, collect fabric samples, draw and doodle in spare moments. Notice how one colour looks good against another. Jot it down in your sketch book; use crayons or dabs of paint to remind you of the precise shade. Go to galleries and museums and discover what colours and shapes other cultures use. Consider ideas and images that are important in your life and incorporate them in your designs. The better prepared you are, the easier the ideas will come.

There are a lot of techniques in this book but don't be alarmed! You don't need to master all of them. But if you try them all, you'll find one which will spark you off. Once you've got your personal means of expression, stay with it. Most of the projects explained in the book can be painted, printed or dyed. Choose the technique that you enjoy most and adapt it to your choice of project.

Materials & Equipment

The materials you will need for painting on fabric can be divided into three sections: fabric, fabric pens, paints and dyes, and additional equipment for each technique, such as pencils, scissors, sponges and frames.

Much of this equipment can be found around the house or else made up quite simply.

When you've acquired your materials, all you need then is a small area in which to work, a flat work surface, some plastic sheeting for protection, an iron and a sink!

Fabric

BEFORE YOU START PAINTING YOU NEED SOME fabric to paint on. When you are looking for fabric in the shops, think about what exactly you want to make and ask yourself the following questions. Does the fabric have to be hardwearing? Will it need frequent washing? Do you want the fabric to be worn? Is there going to be a light source behind it? Try to take into account the thickness, weight, texture and colour when choosing the right fabric for your project.

Curtains need a medium to heavyweight closely woven fabric. Are you going to line them? Will the fabric hang well?

Tablecloths should be made from a medium to heavyweight cotton fabric. Food and drink might be spilled onto it. Will the fabric be easy to wash and iron?

Table mats are best made in medium to heavy-weight cotton or linen. How will they be padded? Are they easy to clean?

Bed linen will be subjected to many washes so medium to lightweight cotton sheeting is the best fabric to buy.

Roller blinds are best made with a medium cotton plain-weave fabric which can be treated with a special fabric stiffener.

Cushions can be made from hardwearing, un-crushable, light, medium and heavy cottons, linens and silk.

Lampshades are best made from light and medium cotton fabric or silk to allow the light to glow through.

Clothing needs to be washable and durable, so choose light or medium cotton or silk.

Buy a little more fabric than you need so you can experiment on test pieces to see how your colours react before you begin your project.

NATURAL FIBRES

Natural fibres are the best for fabric painting, printing and dyeing. All the dyes used in this book are suitable for cotton, silk, wool and linen. If you prefer, you can paint and print on man-made fabrics but the appropriate dyes must be used to get good results.

Natural fibres are divided into cellulose (plant fibres) or protein (animal fibres). Cellulose fibres include cotton, linen and viscose rayon. Protein fibres include silk and wool. Some dyes are more vivid on cellulose than protein fibres and vice versa.

Before you choose the fabric for a project it is essential to establish whether your fabric is made from natural or man-made fibres. A simple test to ascertain its composition is to take a small piece of the fabric and hold it to a naked flame. The man-made fibre will burn easily, give off fumes and will leave a hard, black, plastic residue. The natural fabric will burn slowly and stop as soon as you remove it from contact with the flame. Fabric paints have been developed to suit either types of material but are richer on natural fibres.

It is better to choose white, cream or pale-coloured fabrics for painting on because colour responds more truly. Avoid dark-coloured fabric, unless your paints have strong enough pigments to show up. Dyes also react differently according to the base colours of your fabric. Test them before you start.

FABRICS FOR PRINTING

The following list of fabrics will give you a rough idea of what to look for. It is impossible to mention every type on the market but I have tried to itemize the ones that you might wish to use for the projects in this book. Using the appropriate fabric for your project will help you achieve the best results.

COTTON

Calico can be light, medium or heavyweight, and white or creamy coloured (unbleached cotton). It is cheap, tough and hardwearing. Calico is suitable for the techniques of painting, sponging, stencilling and dyeing, but the creamy colour dulls the tone of the dye.

Cambric is a fine, soft and smooth, lightweight cotton. It dyes well but is too thin for most household items.

Canvas is a heavy, hardwearing, unbleached fabric. It is good for handpainting but not for dyeing. It can be used for deck chairs and floor coverings.

Cotton is excellent for fabric painting. It is hardwearing, can be boiled or bleached, and is easy to cut, sew and dye. When buying your fabric, check that it is pure cotton as nowadays many manufacturers mix cotton with other fibres to make the fabric easier to wash and handle. It is usually reasonably priced but some qualities are as expensive as silk.

Damask is an elegant and hardwearing fabric, but it crushes easily. It is a good fabric for the techniques of printing and dyeing, and is recommended for table linen.

Holland is a firm, hardwearing, plain-weave fabric. It is excellent when stiffened for roller blinds. It is good for printing on, but not so suitable for dyeing.

Lawn is a lightweight, fine, smooth fabric but tends to be expensive. It is suitable for dyeing, printing, batik and marbling, and ideal for clothing and cushions.

Muslin is a soft, sheer, lightweight cotton imported from the Far East. Being an open-weave fabric, muslin lends itself well to net curtains. It is suitable for most painting techniques.

Percale is a close-weave, medium-weight fabric which is hardwearing and smooth. It is available in a variety of widths and is suitable for the techniques of printing, painting and dyeing, and recommended for bed linen.

Poplin is a hardwearing, smooth fabric, similar to percale. It is good for printing and dyeing and suitable for bed linen.

Primissima is a smooth, close-weave, lightweight cotton. It is excellent quality for batik and all kinds of printing and dyeing.

Silk cotton is 50 per cent silk, 50 per cent cotton, and machine-washable. It is an ideal fabric for lightweight clothing and is good for the techniques of printing and dyeing.

Voile is a soft, smooth, semi-transparent, lightweight fabric. It is good for the techniques of printing, painting and dyeing.

SILK

Silk is a natural fibre produced by silkworms. It has a wonderful luxurious look and feel to it and is often mixed with other fibres to make quality fabrics. It is strong and absorbs paint well, making it ideal for fabric painting. Special silk dyes are needed to enhance the delicate, translucent quality of the fabric. Most silks are perfect for printing, painting and dyeing.

Crêpe de Chine is a light, medium and heavy-weight plain-weave silk. It is luxurious and lustrous and hangs beautifully. It is expensive but lovely to work on. Suitable for all fabric painting techniques, crêpe de Chine is excellent for clothing, scarves and cushions.

Doupion is available in different weights and has a high shine and uneven texture, which is ideal for handpainting. It is suitable for clothing and home furnishings.

Habutai is a light, medium and heavyweight, smooth-textured silk. It is excellent for painting, printing and dyeing techniques, and suitable for making scarves, fashionwear, cushions and lampshades.

Shantung is a fine to medium-weight, beautifully textured silk with a delicate sheen. The slub effect adds interest to its surface. It is suitable for all techniques.

Taffeta comes in different weights, it has a smooth-textured surface, and is occasionally woven in two colours to create a luxurious sheen. Taffeta is expensive to buy and is used mainly as an evening dress fabric as it rustles when moved. It can, however, be used for making cushions. It is suitable for all printing and painting techniques, but bleeding effects can occur. This can, however, add to the decorative effect.

Tussah/wild silk is a thick, uneven-textured fabric. It lacks the lustre of other silks, but is good for printing on.

Twill is a fine to medium-weight fabric with a diagonal weave. It is suitable for all printing and painting techniques and can be used for scarves, ties and cushions.

Voile is a creamy, rough-textured fabric. It is suitable for the technique of printing and is ideal for cushion covers.

OTHER NATURAL FABRICS

Linen is a natural fibre made from flax and can be light, medium and heavyweight. It is expensive, and creases badly (but this is considered part of its charm). Linen has a visible weave which makes it ideal for the techniques of painting, sponging, stencilling, marbling and dyeing. It is suitable for clothing and home furnishings.

Velvet comes in a variety of thicknesses and qualities – silk, cotton and polyester. It is a pile cloth. Velvet is suitable for painting and dyeing techniques, but always remember to use silk paints on silk velvet.

Wool comes in different weaves and weights. It is warm and soft, and suitable for the techniques of sponging, stencilling, marbling and especially dyeing. Some weaves are smooth enough to be painted on. It is good for soft furnishings. Do not tumble dry.

▶ When choosing fabric for your project, take into account the thickness, weight, texture and colour of the fabric. Using the appropriate fabric will help you to achieve the best results.

Shantung

Voile

Damask

Cambric

Silk

Calico

Doupion

Percale

Lawn

Cotton

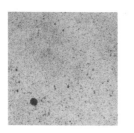

Fabric paints

THERE IS A WIDE VARIETY OF FABRIC PAINTS on the market today and most of them are easy to use. All the fabric paints/inks that I have used in this book are water-soluble, odourless and non-toxic and are suitable for natural fabrics. They are washable too, provided that they have been properly heat-set or steamed, depending on the paints. Different types of fabric paints react on material in different ways. Some sit on the surface of the cloth while others soak in. Different dyes bond with fibres in different ways too. The selection of a colourant will depend on the type of fabric you use, the desired colour scheme, the intended function and the maintenance and the durability of the finished article.

Acrylic paint This can be used on any fabric but tends to sit on the surface if it is not thinned down with water. It does not need any fixing.

Fabric dyes These are used mainly in the second part of the book, both for dyeing fabric which has been batiked and for colouring large pieces of material. I use both *cold water dyes* and *cold water fibre-reactive dyes*. The dye colours are exceptionally clear and have excellent fastness to light and washing. They are readily available from craft shops and may be adapted for dipping as well as for direct application. These are excellent for natural fibres, especially cotton and viscose rayon fabrics, and are fixed with an alkali-soda ash or washing soda crystals. Please read the instructions when making up the dyebath and take particular care when handling the dye powder. The reactive dyes can also be discharged with bleach to give different colours. Again, ensure you take precautions.

Fabric paints These can be used on most fabrics and are unaffected by light, washing or dry-cleaning. There is a good range of colours on the market and colours can be mixed to create even more. Transparent, opaque, pearlized and fluorescent fabric paints are available, as well as glitter paint. The paints can be diluted with water, but if you don't want the paint to spread you can use it straight from the jar. Fabric paints generally sit on the surface of the fabric and do not penetrate the fibres. They are non-toxic and are heat-fixed by ironing for several minutes.

Fabric pens and crayons Fabric pens look like ordinary felt pens except that they are specially designed to be used on fabric. They are clean and easy to control, especially if you want a fine line or dots. They are also fade-resistant and washable. Felt pen markers specially made for fabrics are available with thick, thin and wedge-shaped tips. Some can be refilled. Both pens and crayons are easy to use and are ideal for children. Be careful not to smudge the fabric crayons when drawing on the fabric. Fix the colours by ironing but cover the drawing with a clean cloth so that the iron is protected from greasy marks. You can combine both the fabric pens and crayons with fabric paints to give a more interesting effect.

Oil-based inks These are used for marbling. You can either blend your own with a little white spirit or you can buy ready-made marbling inks.

Silk paints These are easy to use. They are water-soluble before fixing and can be applied to the silk with a brush or sponge. They are transparent and have a translucent quality to them. They can be thinned with water and can be mixed together to create other colours. Because silk paints are more fluid than fabric paints, precise lines or shapes are difficult to achieve. You need to thicken the paint

▶ Fabric paints can be painted onto fabric with a brush (top left), applied with a natural sponge (top right), applied over starch paste (bottom left) or used to flood areas of silk (bottom right).

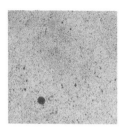

or use gutta or wax to contain the colour. You can also use a diffusing agent to stop hard lines from appearing when painting large areas with a brush.

Some silk paints need to be fixed by ironing, others are fixed by steaming and some have to be immersed in a fixative solution. Read the manufacturer's instructions carefully before you use them. Iron-fixed dyes are easy to use but I prefer to use steam-fixed dyes as the colours are more vibrant. The dyes can be fixed in a pressure cooker or you can send the fabric to a steaming service (see page 78 for address). When using gutta resist make sure the silk paints are compatible with the barrier fluid. Gutta can be water based or spirit based; some dyes are not so good with water-based gutta.

Spray paint The spray paint that flower arrangers use is suitable for use with stencils. Car spray is also good but it tends to make the surface of the fabric a little stiff.

Light-sensitive paints There are now available on the market some transparent paints that react to the sun. You can use them diluted with up to 2 parts water. Dampen the fabric, apply the paint with a brush, lay a mask of feathers, leaves, paper shapes, or lace on the top and allow the fabric to dry in the sun. The areas of the fabric that are uncovered go darker. Iron the fabric to prevent any further change.

PAINT & DYE APPLICATORS

Diffuser This is a metal gadget used to spray dye onto silk by blowing through it.

Printing rollers These are for rolling out the printing ink.

Brushes You will need watercolour brushes of different sizes, paintbrushes and sponge brushes.

Sponges These can give a more textured paint surface.

Pipettes or eye droppers (see Marbling, page 17).

Cotton buds or a clothes peg holding a wad of cotton wool. Use these for applying either a small or a large area of paint or dye.

RESISTS OR DISCHARGE SUBSTANCES

Silk outliners There are two types of gutta – one which is washable, and the other which is mainly spirit based (see Gutta, page 18).

Diluent (sometimes known as dilutant or diffusant) This solution helps the even spreading of dyes.

Antifusant This inhibits the flow of silk paints. Choose the appropriate one supplied by the manufacturers. The colours can be controlled by painting the liquid onto the stretched silk beforehand and then allowing it to dry. Use this if you want to paint fine lines or details (see Freehand painting, page 30). You can also dilute water-based gutta and sponge it over the surface of the fabric. Allow it to dry and then paint the dye on but do not saturate the surface of the silk. Alternatively, try spraying the surface of the silk with hairspray. Let it dry and paint on the surface as usual.

Masking fluid This can be painted onto fabric to mask or resist certain areas of the design from the dye. It can be rubbed off afterwards.

Paste resist You can use paste on fabric to resist direct painting of dye (see page 65 for recipe).

Wax (see Batik materials, page 18).

Alcohol This can be used for pushing the dye around the silk (see Freehand painting, page 30). Use an appropriate manufacturer's alcohol or try methylated spirits, surgical spirit or isopropyl (available from chemists). You will get the best results using steam-fixed dyes, but it is worth experimenting with water-based dyes too.

Salt Try sprinkling table salt, rock salt or sea salt onto wet paint – it attracts and absorbs moisture and creates interesting patterns. It is especially effective when painting on silk.

Bleach This can be used for discharge dyeing. Mix 1 part bleach to 3 parts water if you want a strong solution or 1 part bleach to 5 parts water if you want a normal solution. It may be used on cotton, linen and rayon but should never be used on silk or wool. Take care when using bleach. Avoid splashing it and use a synthetic brush to apply it.

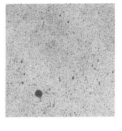

Additional equipment

ALONG WITH THE FABRIC AND DYES, YOU WILL also need some of the following equipment for painting on fabric. Do try to *make do* with objects that can be found around your home. Once you are sure you would like to develop the technique further then you can spend a little money on more expensive equipment.

POTATO PRINTING
Potato, swede or turnip to print with.
Knife to carve or to cut out shapes with.

LINO CUTS
Linoleum This is available from craft shops in different sizes, unmounted or mounted on blocks of wood. It is flat, cheap, strong and washable. It has no grain and can be cut in any direction. For printing on fabric, glue the lino on a block of plywood about 2cm (¾in) thick.
Lino cutting tools You will need V-shaped and U-shaped cutters of various sizes, with a handle.
Printing rollers These are for rolling the printing ink on a glass slab.
Water-based block printing ink This is available in tubes and tubs, and can be used for potato, leaf, block and lino prints.

STENCILLING
Stencil paper You can use special linseed-soaked stencil papers, card, flexible acetate, or low-tack masking tape.
Stencil knife Any sharp-pointed craft knife or single-edged razor blade will do.
Stencil brush Special stencil brushes work best, but any round, stiff bristle brush will do. Use masking tape to bind around a bristle brush. The stubby end can be used as an effective, but cheap, stencil brush.

Spray with a diffuser This is used with dyes for spraying through a stencil.

MARBLING
Oil-based paints or **water-based fabric dyes** There are also a number of marbling colours on the market.
Pipettes and **eye-droppers** These are used for applying drops of paint onto the base. Use a different dropper for each colour.
Marbling tray This is for holding the thick base on which the paints are floated. It should be about 8cm (3¼in) deep and is available from art and photographic suppliers. A pet litter tray can also be used as a marbling tray.
Marbling base The consistency of the base is crucial to the success of the marbling. Various thickening agents can be used – wallpaper paste and carragheen moss (Irish seaweed) are both suitable. You can also buy various marbling base sizes from craft shops.
Patterning tools You can use skewers, tooth-picks, cocktail sticks or wide-toothed combs. Or you can make your own comb by hammering nails into wood or sandwiching pins in between layers of cardboard.

RESIST DYEING
Plastic bowls and **buckets** suitable for small dyebaths. If you need to dye a large amount of fabric, the best idea would be to look for an old sink or large plastic containers and trays from a hardware or DIY shop.
Measuring spoons and **jugs.**
Dye powder kept in clean, clearly labelled screw-top jars.
Plastic clothes pegs and a plastic-coated clothes line.

GUTTA

Gutta resist solution This is a thin, glue-like substance which is applied to fabric, usually fine silk, to create a barrier that keeps the paint within defined areas. It is usually applied with a pipette. There are two types of gutta – water soluble and spirit based. If the gutta is too thick it will sit on the surface of the fabric and not penetrate it to create the barrier; if too thin, it will spread and not be waterproof. Water-based gutta can be diluted with a little water, and spirit-based gutta with the appropriate diluent. Gutta is now available in clear, gold, silver, black and other colours. Coloured gutta lines will remain in the fabric even after washing (but not dry-cleaning) while clear gutta washes out leaving a white outline. Be aware of this when planning your design.

If you are a beginner to silk painting, it is easier to use the water-soluble gutta as it can be washed out of the silk after the dyes have been steam-set. But as you become more experienced you will find that repeated application of dye and alcohol can break down the water-based gutta line. Also, when you over-dye colours, the water-soluble resists tend to lift some of the colour out of the silk when they are removed, leaving a lighter line of colour.

Gutta bottles with nozzle These are necessary for the gutta technique. The bottles are filled with the liquid gutta and have a small metal nib specially designed for the end of the nozzle. Before you start, nip off the tip of the bottle and slip the metal nib into the spout. If necessary, keep the nib in place with masking tape. When the gutta fluid is squeezed, the fluid runs onto the fabric through the fine hole at the end of the metal nib. The nibs come in three different sizes: the lower the number the finer the hole. Gutta nibs are usually sold with a fine copper wire pushed into the spout to prevent the gutta from drying and blocking the spout. Remember to replace the wire inside the metal nib when you have finished using it.

Frame A frame is essential for some of the techniques. It keeps the fabric taut and raised above the surface of the table when you apply the colour or wax. The fabric can be secured to the frame with tape or silk pins. You can make your own frame or you can buy 'slot-in' frames from a craft supplier. You can even use an old picture frame (soft wood, if possible).

Silk or **map pins** These are used to pin the fabric onto the frame. Don't use drawing pins as they can leave large holes in the fabric.

BATIK

Wax heater This can be either a thermostatically-controlled wax pot, an electric frying pan, or a double saucepan on an electric ring.

Wax Many craft shops sell ready-prepared batik wax in the right proportions for general batik work. It usually comes in granulated or bead form and is easy to use. Or you can mix your own batik wax by combining beeswax with paraffin wax. The amount of crackle can be controlled to a certain extent by the composition of the mixture. The more beeswax there is in the recipe, the fewer cracks and more pliable the work will be. The more paraffin, the more crackling will occur and the more brittle the work will be. (This is good for the characteristic crackle effect associated with batik.) A good all-purpose mixture is to use $\frac{3}{4}$ paraffin wax to $\frac{1}{4}$ beeswax. Usually wax for batik is paraffin wax, a mixture of paraffin wax and beeswax or a mixture of 1 part paraffin wax, 1 part beeswax and 1 part microcrystalline wax (a synthetic wax which is cheaper than beeswax but with similar qualities).

Canting (pronounced tjanting) This is a special Javanese tool for applying the wax. It consists of a small copper container or reservoir for the melted wax and a little spout or spouts through which it

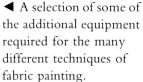

pours onto the fabric. The handle is made of wood. The spout diameter may vary greatly. If you want to draw controlled, fine lines or dots onto the material, choose a finer spout.

Wax brushes There is a range of brushes of different sizes for applying the wax. The brush is an excellent tool for this job. It should be a natural hair or bristle brush rather than a synthetic material. For small lines and detailed work, a pointed sable brush or a Chinese-type watercolour brush is very good. Never leave the brushes in the wax for a long time as they will soon become misshapen and will begin to lose their bristles.

Frame see Gutta above.

MISCELLANEOUS

Palettes You need these to mix paints in. If unavailable, use small plates or saucers instead.

Empty jam jars or **yoghurt pots** These can be used as water containers or for mixing reactive dyes to paint onto fabric.

Applicators You can use the following: brushes, cotton buds, printing rollers and sponges.

Drawing equipment These are all useful: pens, pencils, erasers, ruler, white drawing paper, tracing paper, black felt pen for making outlines bolder before tracing a design.

Kitchen rolls, rags, masking tape All of these are an absolute must.

Miscellaneous equipment Hair dryer, paper and fabric scissors, craft knife, cutting board and card.

Fabric marking water-soluble pen This is a fibre tip pen that marks with a purple or blue line. The line disappears when water touches it, so you can draw directly on the fabric with it.

Glass slab This is a piece of glass with rounded edges and is for rolling the printing ink on.

◄ A selection of some of the additional equipment required for the many different techniques of fabric painting.

Techniques of Surface Painting

In this section you will be introduced to a variety of techniques of *applying paint to the surface* of fabrics. Some are simple and can be successfully tackled by anyone, whatever their skills or abilities. For others, you will need to be more methodical in your approach, or more imaginative in your use of colour. There are no limits to the ideas that can be developed. Follow the instructions, enjoy exploring the different techniques and you will be amazed and proud of your finished results – your very own masterpieces!

Transferring designs onto fabric

MANY PEOPLE LACK CONFIDENCE IN THEIR artistic ability and when it comes to creating designs they don't know how to start. But if you look around you, there is a reservoir of source material and ideas. If you jot down your observations and start to draw you will begin to transfer those ideas onto paper and then onto fabric.

CREATING DESIGNS

Ideas for designs and patterns can be inspired by the most ordinary objects in your home. Look around your kitchen, for example. Unusually shaped objects, cooking utensils, fruit and vegetables can all be sources for designs. Sketch the whole or part of them. Then simplify them by outlining the predominant shapes. Cut out the shapes in card and use them as templates. Draw around them, making repeat patterns. Turn them upside down or reverse them. Try different colour schemes. Vary the tones or scale of the image. Notice the patterns created by the background or negative spaces that link the shapes together. All these ideas can spark off designs for borders, repeat or circular patterns, and can be transformed to produce interesting images.

Once you have transformed an idea into a design or motif, then you have to transfer your design onto an appropriate fabric. This can be done in a variety of ways depending on the project or technique you intend to do. Some people prefer to draw directly onto the fabric, while others prefer to sketch a design onto paper and then transfer it onto fabric by one of the following methods.

Tracing through If the design is the size you want and if your fabric is a light colour and reasonably transparent, like silk or cotton lawn, you can place the pattern under the cloth and, using a soft pencil or water-erasable pen, trace the design exactly. If you can't see the design on the paper very clearly then go over the lines of the drawing with a black pen to make it easier to trace.

Using a window or light box Tape your design to the window and place the fabric over it. The light outside will help you to see the design clearly. Using a soft pencil or water-erasable pen, trace the lines onto the fabric. If you have access to a light box, you will find the strong light source a considerable asset. Place your design and fabric over the light box and trace the lines.

Tracing directly Trace the design directly onto the silk with gutta, following the lines of your drawing.

Cutting templates If you want to create a simple repeated design, use paper or card templates. Make a template by tracing the pattern onto card and then cutting it out. Pin the template onto the printing fabric and draw around the shape with a water-erasable pen.

Dressmaker's carbon paper This is available in several colours, depending on whether you are working on a light or dark fabric. Trace your design onto the paper in the usual way, then place the carbon paper on your fabric, coloured-side down, with the tracing on top. Draw over the lines. Or use a dressmaker's wheel. Follow the line and fine dots will appear on the fabric.

Iron-on transfer paint Paint your design onto cartridge paper and leave to dry. Once dry, place the image face-down on your fabric, and gently iron over the paper. Take care that the paper does

not move and cause smudging while you are ironing it. Remember that the image is reversed.

'Prick and pounce' Trace your design onto tracing paper. Using a darning needle, pierce holes at regular, short intervals along all the lines. Place the pin-pricked paper in position on your fabric. Crush up a piece of tailor's chalk until it becomes a fine powder and sprinkle it over the design, gently brushing it through the holes with a soft brush. Carefully remove the paper, keeping the fabric absolutely flat so as not to disturb the powdered dots lying on the surface. Draw over these with a water-erasable pen or tailor's chalk, joining the dots to form your original drawing.

If you want to repeat the design, use the pierced paper again and again, wiping the underside each time to remove any lingering traces of chalk. This is a good method of transferring designs onto dark fabric.

Tissue paper and thread Trace your design onto tissue paper and pin it onto the fabric. Following the lines, sew small running stitches through the paper and fabric and fasten off securely. When you've finished, gently tear away the tissue paper to reveal the transferred image. This is another good method of transferring designs onto a dark background.

HINTS
● If you use a water-erasable pen, do test it out on the fabric before starting a project.
● In order to prevent blurred images, pin, tape or weight the design securely to the fabric to ensure a clear line and copy of your design.

ENLARGING OR REDUCING A DESIGN
If your design is too small or too big then you will have to either enlarge it or reduce it before you can transfer it onto your fabric. The quickest method of doing this is by using a photocopier. If you have access to one that has enlarging and reducing

capabilities then do take advantage of these.

Alternatively you can use the traditional method of scaling a design up or down. Draw a grid on your design and divide it into equal-sized squares. Take another piece of paper the size you want your design to be. Rule lines to divide this paper into the same number of equal squares as you have in your first drawing. Now follow the squares very carefully, redrawing the design over the second grid. Make sure your pencil crosses the ruled lines at exactly the same points on both charts. You can use the same method to reduce or enlarge a design.

PATTERN-REPEATING A MOTIF
Most of the designs in the printing section of this book start with single motifs. To print a large area of fabric, you need to repeat your motif a number of times. Different effects can be achieved depending on the way the motifs are printed. Images or motifs can be printed randomly, so there is no formal repeat. Or they can be repeated in a formal network pattern of stripes, checks, half-drops, diamonds or within a border of a square or circular design. Whatever pattern you choose, mark out the grid of repeats by stretching threads across the fabric or drawing lines with tailor's chalk. (If you are screen printing, mark your screen at the edges to correspond to the repeats. This is called registration.)

The spaces between the prints often become an important part of the design, or you can create motifs that will interlock so that it is impossible to determine where one ends and the next one begins. (Both lino cuts and screen prints can be designed this way.) Finally, your patterns can be varied even more, by changing tones and colours of the fabric paint or by overprinting (as long as the first print is dry). Printing on different-coloured backgrounds or on a ready-printed fabric can also add strength to a design.

Understanding colour

WHEN YOU START PAINTING ON FABRIC YOU soon discover a lot about colour, such as how one colour works in relationship to another, how colours work in relationship to textures and the space within the design, and how they affect us and our well-being. You might be lucky and have an instinctive approach to choosing colours. You just *feel* that a certain colour has an affinity with another. But it can help if you have some understanding of the basics of colour theory before you start creating your own interesting colour combinations.

MIXING COLOURS

Make a colour wheel, starting with the three *primary colours* or hues★ – red, yellow and blue. (Primary colours are colours that cannot be obtained by mixing.) If you mix two primary colours together you will get a *secondary colour*; red and yellow make orange; blue and yellow make green; and red and blue make purple. That is the theory. In practice you will find it is not always the case. Not all reds when mixed with a blue will make a purple. Some reds are too orangy and will turn the blue into a muddy, brown colour. You need to know which red to use before you can get a good purple. It is the same with the blues and yellows. A bluish-red and violet-blue will produce a clear purple, a greenish-yellow and a turquoise-blue will produce a green, while a yellowish-red and golden-yellow an orange.

So when you buy paints or dyes, it is better to buy two kinds of reds (a slightly orangy-red and a slightly bluish-red), two blues (a slightly violet-blue and a slightly greenish turquoise-blue), and two yellows (a slightly greenish-yellow and a golden-yellow). From these you can obtain any colour that you might wish. If you add black and white to the list, then you can also mix any tint★ or shade★ you need. In the end you will save money by mixing your own colours rather than by buying lots of ready-mixed shades.

A ★ **hue** is a pure colour such as red or orange.
A ★ **tint** is lighter than a hue. It is a term for a hue plus a percentage of white.
A ★ **shade** is deeper and darker than a hue. It is a term for a hue plus a percentage of black.

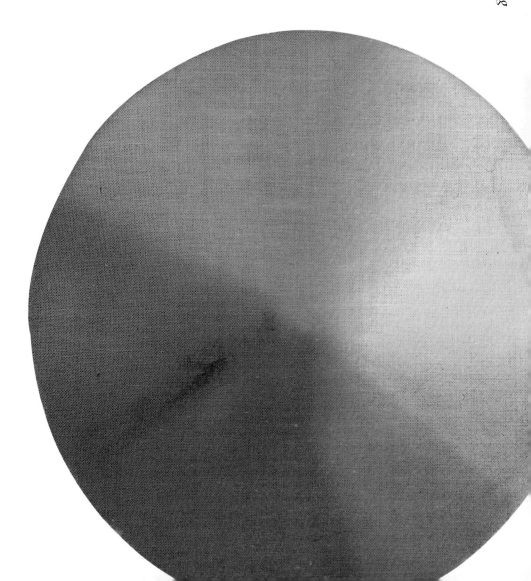

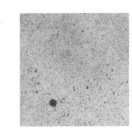

But what colour should you mix? What colours go well with each other? What effect do you want to create? Sometimes you only want to find a colour to blend in with the decor in a room. At other times you want to create an impact.

Creating your own interesting colour combinations is a skill that can be developed but you must begin to understand the different qualities of colours. Colours often influence each other so that the intensity, tone and hue can change. A green on a black will show up lighter and more luminous than against a white background. A tomato next to a green stem will appear redder than if it was next to a purple iris. Different sources of light can also affect the tones of colour. And transparent dyes can be laid over each other creating harmonious tonal shades. If you are worried about combining a variety of hues, limit yourself to tones of one or two colours only. But take your cue from nature. Look closely at a stone wall or a stump of a tree or the head of a flower and you will be amazed at the range of colours that are contained within a small area. Certain colours that you did not think could 'go' together, do.

Analagous colours (those which are near to each other in the colour wheel) often look rich and vivid together. See how the yellow, yellow-orange, orange, red-orange and red on the colour wheel react with each other. You cannot go wrong using analagous colours because they are so closely related and seem to harmonize with each other.

Also *complementary colours* (which are opposite from each other on the colour wheel) can look brighter and more intense if they are next to each other. The contrast of the colours is strengthened, as you can see in nature, for example a purple pansy with a yellow centre or a red rose with green leaves. Red is the complementary of green, yellow of purple and blue of orange. Even tertiaries and the tints and shades of a colour have complementary colours. So a red-orange is complementary to a greenish-blue and pink is complementary to a pale green. A small amount of complementary colour will liven up a colour scheme.

Complementary colours can be mixed with each other to make neutral greys. These are more subtle and muted than the steely greys you get when you mix black and white. They are also extremely effective if you want to tone down a dominant colour in your design. Add a little green to a glaring red and the red will become less predominant.

EVOKING MOOD

Colours can evoke different moods. Certain colours *feel* warm and others cool. Warm colours are yellows, reds, oranges and some pinks. Cool colours are in the blue-green range. Whether a colour is seen as cool or warm depends also to a large extent on the surrounding colours. A greenish-blue, for example, might look cold on its own but considerably warmer next to a pink. On the whole, warm colours come forward and are useful for the dominant areas of the design while cool colours recede and are better in the background.

ADDING CONTRAST

When designing a colour scheme, try to achieve some tonal contrast in your design. Colours of an equal tone can look good together, but sometimes a little contrast or sparkle is needed to add more interest to your colour scheme. Add contrasting dark or light tones to emphasize different parts of the design. Vary the proportion of dark to light and light to dark. For example, when you have a range of blue tones, add the odd orange one to create extra interest. But don't overdo it. The more colours that are in a composition the more difficult it is to achieve colour balance. It is more successful to let one colour dominate in a pattern.

When you have experimented with mixing colours, jot them down on paper. Record how you mixed a particular tone so you can refer to it at a later date. This will save you a lot of time when deciding on colours for a certain project.

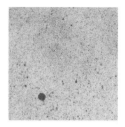

Fixing methods for paints & dyes

FABRIC PENS, CRAYONS, PAINT, INKS AND DYES all need to be fixed permanently into the silk or cotton so the colours won't run when the item is washed. When you buy the paints or dyes, check the method of fixing before you use them. Some of the colours and dyes need to be fixed by heat, usually by ironing, while others are fixed by steaming or by a liquid solution.

Felt pen markers and **fabric crayons** are usually fixed by heat, either by ironing on the wrong side for five minutes or by heating in an oven. Remember to place a piece of waste cloth between your iron and the design, to avoid getting wax on the surface of the iron.

Silk dyes can often fade or become marked if they are not fixed properly. Transparent dyes usually need to be immersed in a fixative solution or steam-fixed. Opaque silk paints are fixed with ironing or with the heat of a hair dryer. There are some dyes on the market, however, that don't need to be fixed in the usual way. Just let them dry in the air naturally.

Iron-fixing Make sure the silk dyes are completely dry and then iron on the reverse side for about five minutes. You can usually iron directly onto the silk but if you are concerned that the dyes or gutta might mark the iron or ironing board then protect the silk with a clean cloth.

Liquid solution Make sure the silk is dry before soaking it in the solution for over an hour. Then rinse the silk in warm water to remove any fixative and dry. You can also steam-fix silk that has been dipped in liquid solution.

Steam-fixing If you are dyeing only a small amount of silk, try steaming it in a pressure cooker. Place each piece of silk flat on several layers of lining paper or porous, brown wrapping paper (not shiny). Do not use newspaper as the print will mark the silk. Roll the first piece of silk and paper together, smoothing out any creases. Do not place the silk too close to the edges of the paper. Flatten and seal the ends with tape that can withstand moisture. Tuck the ends in towards the centre and roll the silk and paper into a small firm package.

Fill the bottom of the pressure cooker with water to the depth of 2–3cm ($\frac{3}{4}$–1$\frac{1}{4}$in). Place the package in a metal basket and suspend it *above* the boiling water. The package should not touch the sides of the pressure cooker as condensation can form on the sides and stain the silk if it is not protected properly. So cover the basket with paper and then a sheet of aluminium foil so that the condensation runs down into the water. Seal the lid and cook under pressure for 45 minutes.

▼ Place a piece of paper or cloth between the iron and the fabric and iron on the reverse side of the fabric for about five minutes to fix the colours.

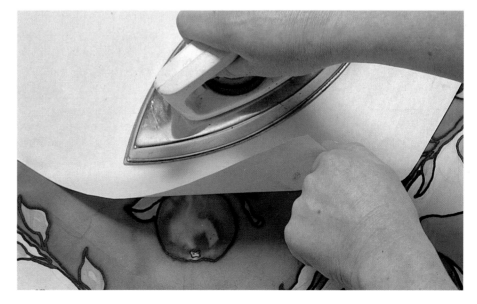

Before you start

PREPARING FABRIC

Before starting each project I will remind you to prepare the fabric, meaning that the fabric must be washed and ironed. It is possible to buy fabric which has been specially prepared for printing and dyeing, which will save you having to wash and iron it yourself. However, most fabric is treated with a special finish which makes it water-resistant and less absorbent and it is therefore important to prepare it.

Wash cotton fabric at a medium to hot temperature with your usual detergent. Iron it while it is still damp so you can remove all the creases. More delicate fabrics like silk and wool should be hand-washed in lukewarm water with a mild detergent. Dampen off the excess water with a towel and then iron while the fabric is still damp. Check that your iron is on a silk setting.

PREPARING TO PAINT

Painting and printing can be a messy business so preparation is most important. Divide your work surface up into sections. It is important that the area in which you want to print is kept free of dyes, paints and brushes – that careless blob of paint can ruin a masterpiece.

Make sure that your printing surface is flat. For the best results, prepare a padded table covered with a washable surface. Spread an old blanket over the table and tack or tape it down so it is taut. To protect the blanket, stretch polythene sheeting over it and secure this as well. Check that there are no wrinkles in your fabric. Secure it to the work surface with masking tape. Keep a washable pencil at hand. Sometimes you will need to sketch out your design on the fabric.

Before you start any of the projects in this book, use this page as a checklist.

- Read the instructions carefully, especially on how to apply and fix the paint or dye. Does it have to be heat-fixed by iron? Or does it need special fixing solution baths or steaming?
- Check you have enough paint and dye. If you run out halfway through a project, you may find matching a colour impossible.
- Check the consistency of the paint. It must be suitable for the technique and for the fabric that is being painted. Test before you begin.
- Don't mix the products as colour and consistency of different brands of paint will vary.
- Have you enough brushes? One for each colour is a good idea. Rinse them thoroughly after use and wipe dry with a clean cloth.
- Keep a jam jar filled with water close by – this is useful to clean brushes. However, don't leave a brush standing in water or it will be ruined.

For inking up your printing blocks, you can use four different methods.

1. Roll thicker fabric paint onto a glass slab and press the block into it, *or*

2. Saturate a piece of felt with fabric paint in a flat dish or tin lid and press the block into that; *or*

3. Fabric paint can be painted on the block with a brush. The advantage of this is that a variety of colours can be applied to the block at the same time; *or*

4. If the block is large enough, roll the fabric paint directly onto it.

With each of these methods, don't use too much fabric paint as the texture of your block can get lost in the printing process. And allow enough time for a print to dry before you print over it.

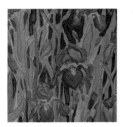

Freehand painting

PAINTING YOUR FABRIC FREEHAND IS PROBABLY the simplest of all fabric painting techniques. You can treat the fabric as a canvas and make marks, create patterns, or paint pictures with just a brush and some fabric paint. Dots, lines, swirls and strokes can all be spontaneous or pre-planned, but use the opportunity to get acquainted with the different fabric paints and dyes and the effects they have on different thicknesses of fabric.

PAINTING ON COTTON OR LINEN
Experiment with small pieces of cotton of various textures and see how different fabric paints react. As long as the paints are of a thick and non-runny consistency, you can control your brushwork and paint pictures or add patterns and borders to a cushion or piece of clothing without any worry of the paint spreading. You can produce any painterly effect, from the most precise detail to the soft flowing quality of transparent watercolour. Mix your colours carefully and don't dilute your paint with too much water because the water often separates from the pigment, leaving streaks and smudges on the fabric.

PAINTING ON SILK
Silk paints can be applied to cotton or synthetic fabrics, but they work especially well on pure silk. They are runnier than fabric paints so they will spread more easily. You can apply resists (see pages 65, 68 and 71) to stop the paint/dye from spreading into other areas. But before you do that explore the different effects you can achieve with the paints on their own. If you want to have more control over your brushwork, coat the silk with an antifusant liquid or thicken the silk paints with a thickener.

The strength, lustre, and durability of silk, combined with its beauty, make it a perfect fabric for painting on. It has a delicate, translucent quality not found in other materials. By using simple techniques you can create subtle and exciting effects. Experiment on small pieces of silk before attempting a wallhanging or picture.

Experimenting with silk painting
Wash, dry and iron the silk, then stretch it over a frame. Experiment on wet and dry silk using both thinned and thick paint. The results will be unpredictable but exciting. Try dripping paint onto the fabric, allowing each drop to run its full extent before continuing. Notice what happens when different colours merge.

Apply the paint with a variety of objects to give different effects, for example, brushes, eye dropper, sponge, screwed-up paper, or cardboard. Make a definite rhythmic pattern of lines, grids or spirals and allow the colours to run into each other. Using a thin brush or a cotton bud, criss-cross with lines of a different colour.

Drip water onto areas of colour and notice how it spreads and pushes the paint. You can also dilute the water with a few drops of alcohol. This accentuates the effect and softens the brilliance of the paints. If you are using steam-fixed dyes you can use alcohol to create more pronounced textures than with water. Apply a droplet of alcohol with a brush or cotton bud to the dyed silk. It will spread into a spot and will push the dye to the outer edge of the spot, creating a thin ring of colour.

Try sponging the fabric with water, and paint on different dyes starting with the lightest colour. While the paint is still wet, sprinkle salt crystals on the fabric. This can be done either in a random way or in patterns. Remove the salt when the paint is completely dry.

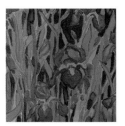

*H*andpainted *hanging*

Now that you are aware of the possibilities of silk painting, combine the techniques and create your own subtle and exciting images. Wallhangings are particularly attractive in rooms because they lend texture, colour and depth to the surroundings. Also the design can add an entirely new dimension to the room.

You will need:
- White silk (medium or heavyweight habotai or crêpe de Chine)
- Masking tape
- Water-soluble pen
- Adjustable frame
- Silk pins
- Silk paints
- Watercolour brushes of different sizes
- Palette or clean saucers
- Alcohol diluent
- Coarse salt
- Cotton buds
- Clean cloth
- Jar of water
- Iron
- Staple gun and staples
- Picture frame, canvas stretcher or 2 battens
- Cord

▶ Using a soft brush so that the silk paints flow smoothly, apply the paints one at a time.

I DON'T EXPECT YOU TO BE ABLE TO COPY THIS hanging exactly as both the silk and dyes you use will dictate to some extent how your picture develops. The fibres of the silk allow the dyes to flow and spread more freely than on watercolour paper. Try incorporating flowers, birds, fish or watery scenes in your design, as silk painting lends itself to natural images.

Here I have chosen to work on silk mainly because it hangs well and will add a luxurious quality to the decor. I also used iron-fixed dyes mainly because they are easier to fix. I allowed the dyes to spread and blend into each other, creating blurred and unusual shapes. I used salt technique on the pond area and painted drops of water and alcohol on the background for a mottled effect.

1 Prepare the silk as explained. Tape the silk flat on the work surface and use a water-soluble pen to sketch the outlines of the irises. Your drawing will disappear as soon as the paints are applied. The paints often create unexpected effects. Be flexible. Using silk pins, stretch the silk taut across the frame.

2 Prepare the colours you are going to use. Blend or dilute the colours in a clean palette or saucers. Ensure you have enough paint for the whole hanging.

3 Apply the paints one at a time, starting with the palest colour. Use a soft brush so that the silk paints flow smoothly. Wash and dry your brush thoroughly between each application. If you want to minimize the bleed effects, leave each colour to dry before applying the next one.

4 *You can use several techniques to create special effects. Allow the dye to spread and dry naturally. Dark ridges of colour will form along the edges of the colour. You can use these wonderful effects in the background.*

5 *Sprinkle coarse salt over the silk while the dyes are still wet. Wavy edges are created as the salt pulls the dye across the surface of the silk. This technique can produce some very interesting and dramatic effects and is especially*

▶ Sprinkle coarse salt over the silk while the dyes are still wet.

good for water. If you use steam-fixed dyes, apply drops of alcohol to create textures for the reeds.

6 *When the silk is completely dry, remove it from the frame and fix the paints by ironing the silk with a medium hot iron, covering it first with a clean piece of fabric so that it does not get marked.*

7 *Finally, either stretch the silk over a frame or stretcher or staple the top and bottom to two battens, attach some cord and hang your masterpiece from a hook.*

◀ The salt pulls the dye across the surface of the silk to create a blotchy, textured effect.

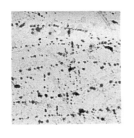

Spatter painting

SPATTER PAINTING IS ANOTHER TECHNIQUE that is simple to do – and you don't have to be a brilliant artist. Think of a Jackson Pollock but on a smaller scale. Colours can be flicked onto fabric using a toothbrush, large paintbrush or stick, depending on the effect desired.

Before you attempt to do any spatter painting, make sure the area surrounding your work surface is well protected. Cover all surfaces with newspaper, a dust sheet or plastic sheeting. If possible work outside as stray blobs of paint can get everywhere. Lay out the fabric on your work surface, smooth it down and secure it in place with masking tape. Dip a brush or stick into your paint and flick the paint onto the cloth by jerking your wrist. Try different arm and wrist movements and see the variety of effects you can achieve. Experiment with small and large brushes on different fabrics. The size of the brush used will determine the quantity of colour applied to the fabric. The larger the brush, the bigger the splash effects. Allow each colour to dry completely before adding another to prevent the colours from merging. It may take some time so be patient.

► Run the end of a paintbrush over a toothbrush laden with paint to produce small spatters on the fabric.

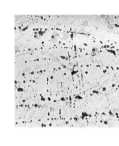

*S*pattered director's chair *(pictured on page 35)*

Having had fun experimenting with the technique of spattering, here's a simple project to try out. Director's chairs are readily available from furniture stores and are fairly inexpensive. The canvas seat and back are detachable, making them ideal for fabric painting. Spattering is a quick and easy technique that will enliven the most ordinary of chairs.

You will need:

- Director's chair with detachable seat and back fabric
- Newspaper or protective sheeting
- Fabric paints of different consistencies
- Clean containers for mixing colours
- Large or medium paintbrushes
- Iron

1 Remove the back support and seat fabric of the director's chair and lay them flat on some newspaper. Make sure the surrounding area is covered satisfactorily with newspaper or other protective sheeting.

2 Prepare the paints in separate containers. Make sure you have enough, as spatter painting tends to use up a lot of colour. If you want a paler colour, dilute the paint with a little water, but don't over-dilute.

3 Start with the lightest colour. Simply dip a brush into the paint and flick the paint onto the chair fabric. Allow the first colour to dry before you apply the next one, otherwise they will merge together and create a blurred effect. Use a different paintbrush for each colour.

4 Once you have applied the darkest colour, allow the paint to dry, then fix the colour by ironing both sides of the canvas with a hot iron, three minutes each side. Keep a cloth between the fabric and the iron, to prevent any paint from sticking to the iron.

5 Re-attach the canvas seat and back support to the frame of the director's chair and try it out!

◀ Flick a paint-laden brush over the fabric to make colourful spatters.

▼ Tap a smaller brush against a stick to produce smaller spatters.

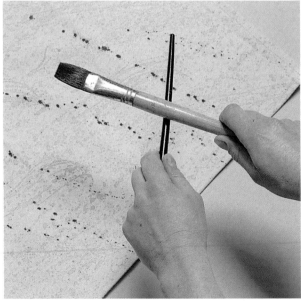

Sponging

SPONGING IS A WONDERFUL WAY OF COVERING a large area quickly. The texture can be a background for further printing or can be a pattern on its own. Use this technique on tablecloths, pillowcases, quilts – even lampshades – for lovely effects.

Most fabrics are suitable for sponging. Decide what kind of effect you would like and then choose the appropriate sponge and fabric paints. Natural sponges are the best for this technique, especially if you want a crisp, spotty effect. If you want a softer and more blurred effect with a regular pattern, then choose a cheaper, man-made foam sponge.

Mix the fabric paints in clean containers and make sure the sponge is clean and dry. Before you start on your final project, do some trial pieces to see how the paint reacts on the fabric. If it spreads too much for the effect you want, then thicken the paint. Experiment and occasionally allow the colours to bleed into each other and form new colours.

APPLYING THE PAINT

Lightly dip the sponge into the paint. Don't put too much paint on the sponge or else the mark the sponge makes will be a thick blob, not a textured surface. Start with the palest colours first and lightly dab the sponge all over the fabric, leaving a gap between each dab. Keep dipping the sponge into the paint as you go. Vary the textures and tones. Wash the sponge and allow it to dry.

Using a clean sponge, apply the second shade of colour and allow the colours to merge to create overlaps and new tones. Continue to apply the layers, gradually getting darker in tone. Once you are satisfied with the overall effect leave the fabric to dry. If you would like to use glitter paints, sponge them on last.

◀ To create more detail in a sponged pattern, use a craft knife to cut away the foam leaving a raised pattern, and sponge in the usual way.

Sponged fabric lampshade

Sponging is an effective paint technique to use on many surfaces, and can cover a large area very quickly. Here you can produce an attractive marbled, textured lampshade in very little time. You could go on to coordinate your bedroom furnishings using the same pattern!

You will need:
- Fabric paints
- Clean saucers
- Natural sponge
- White or pale-coloured fabric lampshade
- Bowl of water
- Paper towels
- Hair dryer

1 Pour the fabric paints into individual clean saucers and lightly dip the sponge into the paint. The sponge must be dry to get the best effects. Test the strength of colour on a piece of scrap fabric.

2 Starting with the palest colour, dab the sponge lightly all over the lampshade leaving some gaps between each dab. Don't press too hard as this can spoil the effect. Vary the tones and textures by dabbing with different areas of the sponge. Rinse the sponge and dry it with paper towels before using the next colour.

3 Once the first sponging is dry, apply the second colour to the lampshade. Fill in the gaps and overlap the previous colour. Again, allow the fabric paint to dry and apply a third colour, stopping when you are happy with your results.

4 Fix the paints by blow-drying the lampshade with a hair dryer. Do this for several minutes but make sure you do not hold the dryer too long in one place otherwise it might burn the shade.

5 You should now have an attractive marbled, textured lampshade. If you want a little more detail on the shade you can cut some latex foam into different designs, and overprint with this. Draw an outline of your design on one side of the foam block. Use a craft knife or sharp scissors to cut away the background, thus leaving a raised pattern. Apply the fabric paint onto the block and print onto the lampshade. The pattern can be bold but will have soft textured edges.

◀ Dip the sponge into the paint, then dab the sponge lightly all over the lampshade, leaving gaps between each dab.

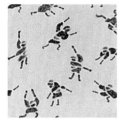

Using markers & crayons

DIRECT PAINTS, FABRIC MARKERS, FABRIC crayons and inks are applied by drawing, painting, printing or spraying directly onto the surface of a natural or man-made fabric. They are non-toxic, easy to use and ideal for creating patterns on clothing and soft furnishings. Do not confuse them with transfer crayons and paints.

Felt pen markers are simple to handle and it is easy to make definite marks and lines with them. Experiment on different fabrics. You could try making lines from one side of the fabric to the other or from top to bottom; make them straight, bent, even, or irregular. Build these up to make borders and all-over patterns. Alternatively, make all-over and linear patterns using dots and circles.

Fabric pastel crayons are like the pastel crayons you use on paper. When you experiment with them you will find they give a much softer and more smudgy line than the felt pen markers. Here are a few ideas you can try.

▼ Lay a piece of thin fabric over a clean shoe sole and rub a crayon over the fabric. The pattern of the sole will be transferred to the fabric.

Grated colours
Use a craft knife or a pencil sharpener to grate some of the crayons onto the fabric. Now cover the fabric with greaseproof paper and iron over the paper so that the crayon shavings melt into each other. The extent to which the shapes and colours change depends on the fabric you have used. Start with a cotton material, then experiment with silk or canvas.

Rubbings
Lay a piece of thin fabric over a hard-textured surface like canvas, metal, glass or string and rub a crayon over the fabric. The pattern of the object beneath will transfer itself to the fabric. It is important to rub the crayon over the material in one direction only, and not backwards and for-wards as you would do with a paper rubbing. Try rubbing over your fabric with more than one colour crayon and with different backgrounds.

Leaves
Rub crayons over the back of leaves where the ribs and veins are most prominent. Place the leaves crayon-side down on the fabric, cover with greaseproof paper and iron over the paper to melt the crayon into the fabric.

Drawing
Draw with the crayon on greaseproof paper, or rub the back of a drawing or photocopy using different-coloured crayons. Place the fabric on a hard surface and turn the paper crayon-side down on the fabric. Use a biro to draw on the back of the paper to transfer the crayon to the fabric.

You can create a composite rubbing using crayons, paints and fabric markers together. Remember to iron the fabric after each application to prevent smudging.

Crayoned canvas shoes (pictured on page 41)

Once you have experimented with the crayons and markers, have a go at decorating some canvas shoes to brighten up your summer wardrobe! This is a great way to renovate old favourites. Draw animals, birds or faces, or go for something jazzy with different-coloured stripes, dots or stars. Remember to match your design on both shoes.

You will need:
- Canvas shoes
- Waste paper
- Fabric crayons/felt pens

1 Scrub the fabric shoes thoroughly with soap and water and then leave to dry before you begin painting.

2 Stuff the insides of the shoes with tissue paper to stretch the fabric smooth. This will make crayoning easier.

3 Using fabric crayons or felt pens, try drawing stripes, squares and squiggles on your shoes. Remember to match or mirror your design on both shoes.

4 If you would like to extend your crayoned design further, you can decorate a canvas shoulder bag to match.

◀ Using fabric felt pens, draw a design onto canvas shoes.

▲ Draw a matching design onto a canvas shoulder bag.

Printing

PRINTING IS ONE OF THE SIMPLEST METHODS of making patterns of colour on fabric. The easiest printing blocks are ones that you can find in the house and garden. They must have a simple flat surface or raised texture. Use natural objects like leaves, bark and vegetables, or man-made ones like sponges, string, polystyrene and cork.

▼ Make simple but effective printing blocks from such man-made objects as string, card and cork.

HOW TO PRINT

Before you begin printing, wash and dry any object you intend to use. This will remove any dirt or grease. Then roll thick fabric paint on a glass slab or soak it into a piece of felt in a flat dish. Either press the object or printing block into the paint or dab the paint onto a block with a sponge or brush. Make sure you do not put too much paint onto the block as it will get messy.

Press the painted object or block onto the fabric, paint-side down, to make a print. The padded table will help to give a good surface. Repaint the object/block and make another print and so on. Sometimes you can get a number of prints from one painting, especially if you want the pattern to become fainter. Print separately or overlap the shapes until you achieve the design you like. When you have finished, leave the paint to dry and then fix by ironing the fabric with a hot iron. Keep a cloth between the iron and the painted fabric, so that the excess paint does not come off on the iron.

BUILT-UP BLOCKS

Once you have exhausted the possibilities of found objects, you may want to make your own printing blocks. To do this, take a small block of wood, about 2.5cm (1in) in depth and build up the printing surface by sticking objects onto it. You can use pieces of card, felt, leather, string, nails, pipe-cleaners, polystyrene, sponges, or coarse-textured fabric like hessian or lace. You can produce wonderful textures and overlapping designs by varying the patterns and colours.

Having had fun experimenting with basic printing, try printing objects together to build up a picture. Ferns can suggest fir trees, sponges can be clouds, while matches or card can be turned into fences or houses. Experiment and see what you can create. Keep to one colour at first and you will find that the textural differences in the printing objects will provide a variety of tone and interest.

Mixed media printed screen

A hand-printed screen can be an attractive focal point in a living room or bedroom. If you have an old screen you can re-cover it in your own designed fabric. Sometimes you can pick up an old screen frame in a second-hand furniture shop. Remove the old covering, hinges, tacks and nails, and sand down the wooden frame before using, if necessary.

You will need:
- Tape measure
- Screen
- Scissors
- Medium-weight cotton fabric
- Pencil and paper
- Masking tape
- Variety of printing objects
- Printing ink
- Glass slab
- Roller and paintbrushes
- Iron
- Clean cloth
- Staple gun and staples
- Decorative studs or tacks
- Braid or wooden beading

1 Measure the height and width of the screen and cut the fabric to fit. You should have eight pieces of fabric of the same size – four for the front of the screen and four for the back. Make sure that you add a few centimetres on each side of the fabric so you can staple it easily onto the frame of the screen once you have finished printing.

2 Plan your designs for the panels on paper. They can be variations of a theme or you can repeat an idea in each panel. Abstract designs can be fun or you may prefer a more figurative approach.

3 Secure the fabric to the table with masking tape. Print the background with muted colours and leave to dry.

To print more definite images, I tore paper shapes and rolled the colour over them onto the background. I then printed shapes using string, card and pipe cleaner blocks, and polystyrene sheets with images drawn on them. I also cut out a paper template of a pyramid and sprayed over it to create pyramid shapes across the screen.

4 Once you have finished printing your designs, allow the paint to dry, then iron the fabric to fix the colour.

5 Starting on the back panels, turn in the edges of the fabric and staple to the frame. Check that the fabric is taut before fixing. Now do the front panels. Fasten in place with evenly-spaced studs or tacks, or decorate with braid or wooden beading. Rehinge the panels together.

▶ A simple method of printing is to roll paint over torn paper shapes placed on a background. Peel off the paper shapes to create an interesting pattern.

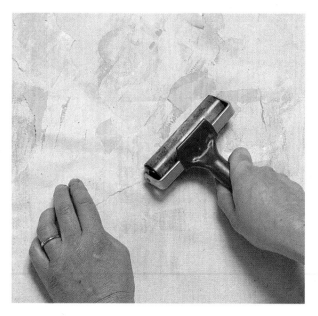

Carved block printing

▼ Carve a simple relief design into the cut surface of half a potato, dry it, then cover it with paint ready for printing.

ANOTHER METHOD OF MAKING PATTERNS OF colour on fabric is to carve a block from wood, rubber, cork, lino or potato to create different designs. The printing surface is cut into with a knife or special gouge to remove the unwanted or white areas of the pattern. The surface is then covered with paint and pressed firmly onto fabric leaving an impression. This is the simplest method of fabric printing, and is traditional in many countries, such as India.

POTATO PRINTS

Vegetable and fruit prints are an effective way of designing fabrics. They can be complete or pieces can be cut out with a knife or gouge. Potatoes are the most commonly used vegetables for printing, though swedes and turnips are also suitable, especially as they are firmer and drier than potatoes.

First wash the potato if necessary, and then cut it in half. Make sure the knife is sharp so it can cut cleanly. Let the potato stand for a time, and then wipe off any excess moisture which might make the print watery.

Cut off any excess potato and carve a simple relief design with a small knife or gouge. The cuts should have a V-section and be as deep and clean as possible. Remember, whatever is cut away will remain white on the print (if the potato is then printed on a white fabric). Dry the potato shape on a paper towel and paint the surface with water-based fabric paint. (Oil-based paint will not print evenly because of the moisture in the potato.) Do not use too much paint or allow it to be too runny. Press the potato firmly onto the fabric. Repeat the prints over the fabric, reapplying paint each time, then leave the fabric to dry. Fix the fabric paints by ironing the fabric with a hot iron. Place a cloth over the fabric so that the excess paint does not come off on the iron.

Should the potato block become too soft and start to lose its shape before the printing is completed, simply recut the design. To do this, make a print on a spare piece of paper and cut it out. Place this print on a newly-cut potato and cut the design again.

Potato-printed floor cushion (pictured on page 47)

Hand-printed floor cushions make a cheap and attractive alternative to conventional furniture. They are also comfortable to sit on when watching television! Use strong, close-woven fabrics to withstand wear and tear.

You will need:
- 90cm (1yd) square of thick cotton, linen, or canvas fabric
- Masking tape
- Knife or gouge
- Potatoes
- Paper towels
- Paintbrushes
- Fabric paints
- Iron
- Clean cloth
- Pins
- Two 92.5cm (37in) squares of cotton lining material
- Sewing machine
- Shredded foam filling
- Matching thread and needle
- 90cm (1yd) square of strong backing fabric
- Scissors
- Zip fastener (optional)

1 Stretch out the fabric on the work surface and fix in place with masking tape.

2 Cut out simple shapes in the potatoes, and print as explained. Build up the design using different tones of colour. The results will look like a mosaic.

3 Allow the fabric paints to dry overnight, then cover the surface with a cloth and iron-fix the fabric paints by ironing over the cloth for five minutes.

4 To make the inner cushion pad, pin the two pieces of cotton lining together, right sides facing. Machine stitch around three and a half sides, and turn right side out. Insert as much of the foam filling as you can through the gap in the stitching. Sew up the gap carefully with small stitches.

5 Pin the backing fabric to the printed fabric, right sides together. Machine stitch around three and a quarter sides of the cushion, leaving a 1.5cm ($\frac{5}{8}$in) seam allowance. Trim the seam edge and clip diagonally across the corners. Turn right side out. Insert a zip fastener in the fourth side, if desired. Or leave a gap big enough to insert the cushion pad and complete the cover with an invisible seam.

◄ Cut a simple shape out of a potato, cover it with paint, and print on the fabric in different colours to build up a design.

Lino cuts

A LINO BLOCK CAN BE USED FOR LARGER AND more complicated designs than a potato. It is flat and cheap, washable and reasonably long-lasting. Although it is easier to cut than wood, you will not be able to produce delicate lines or interesting textures with lino. Most lino-cut designs are composed of relatively large, simple shapes with few intricate lines.

Lino can be bought in different sizes from craft shops. Usually it is unmounted so if you are printing on fabric you should glue your lino onto a wooden block about 3cm (1¼in) thick and the same size as the lino, either before or after the pattern has been cut. This makes it easier to hold both for cutting and printing.

Lino is softer than it used to be, so you shouldn't have any problems cutting it. But should you find it difficult to cut the design, place the lino on the radiator or in a low oven for a few minutes and then it will be less brittle.

▼ Use a V-shaped lino cutting tool to cut shallow trenches in the lino.

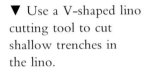

PRINTING THE DESIGN

Make a sketch of the design on paper. Use a pencil to transfer the design to the surface of the lino block but remember to reverse it (especially when you want to print letters) since the lino block is the mirror image of your intended print.

Begin by using a V-shaped lino cutting tool to cut shallow trenches around the areas to be gouged out, then remove larger areas with the larger U-shaped gouge. Be careful to keep both hands behind the cutting edge of your tool. When the cutting is complete, wash the block with warm, soapy water. Dry before printing.

Stretch the fabric onto the work surface and secure the edges with masking tape. Squeeze a small amount of fabric paint/ink onto a glass slab. Use a roller to spread the ink on the glass. When the roller is evenly covered with a thin layer of ink, roll the ink onto the lino block. Two or three inkings are necessary for the first print. The parts that are not cut away will receive the ink. If some of the gouged areas get inked, this means they are not deep enough, so use your cutting tool to gouge out some more of the lino. Make sure you apply the printing ink sparingly – if there is too much the textures of the patterns will disappear when you are printing.

Place the lino face-down onto the fabric. Press firmly or roll over with a clean roller. Lift the block carefully. The print should be quite textured and free of excess ink. Once you are satisfied re-ink the lino block and print it again, allowing enough space between each print.

At first stick to a one-colour design and when you are more confident you can go onto two or three colours, but always begin by printing the lighter colour first. When the printing ink has dried, iron-fix the design.

Lino-cut table napkins

Napkins are always useful to have and are very easy to decorate. You can print some to match tablecloths or place mats. To estimate the fabric required for one napkin, decide its finished size and add 12mm (½in) on each side for hems. To make four napkins 45cm (18in) square, you will need 1m (40in) of fabric, 90cm (36in) wide.

You will need:
- Pencil and paper
- Piece of lino
- Carbon paper
- Lino cutting tools
- Fabric cut to size
- Masking tape
- Fabric paint or water-based printing inks
- Glass slab
- 2 printing rollers
- Scrap paper
- Iron
- Clean cloth
- Needle and thread

1 Draw out your design on a piece of paper and then transfer it to the lino block using carbon paper.

2 Cut out the areas you do not want to print, using V-shaped and U-shaped lino cutting tools. I cut the positive and negative designs in the lino.

3 Ink up the roller with a thin layer of ink and roll the ink onto the lino. Two or three inkings are necessary.

4 Test the first prints on a piece of scrap paper, before printing on the fabric. Print the design onto a corner of the first napkin. Roll a clean printing roller over the back of the lino. Roll more colour onto the lino block and print it onto the material, using an offcut as a space guide.

5 Once all four napkins have been printed, allow to dry. Protect the design with a cloth and iron over the cloth to fix the paint.

6 Finish the raw edges of each napkin by turning in a 6mm (¼in) double hem. Press well and stitch to secure.

◄ Using a printing roller, roll ink onto the lino block then place the lino on the fabric paint-side down and roll a clean printing roller over the back to make the print.

Stencilling

THIS METHOD OF PATTERNING HAS BEEN USED for hundreds of years on wallpapers and borders, fabrics and floors. It is inexpensive, easy to do and can also be a very effective way of repeating a design on fabric. Colour is brushed, sponged or sprayed over a cut-out shape. The shape or template can be cut from thin card, such as a cereal packet, oiled or waxed card, flexible acetate film, or low-tack masking tape, leaving a stencil.

You can buy ready-designed stencils but it is more fun to create and cut your own. Don't make your designs too complicated, and remember that each shape must be connected to the outside edge, or else the pattern simply falls apart.

Before you attempt to cut your own stencils, you should try out some of the following ideas. Experiment first on a sheet of paper and explore the various effects you can achieve with different paints and methods of application:
• Use some natural templates like leaves and simple flower shapes.
• Man-made shapes like metal parts, cogs, screws, bolts and curtain rings can all be arranged to make patterns.
• Some open-weave fabrics like canvas, net and lace curtaining, and other materials like metal or plastic nettings, can create all-over patterns.
• Masking tape can be used to make a variety of criss-cross patterns.
• Paper templates can be made by folding and cutting paper, or using doilies.

Cutting your own templates

Plan a design on a sheet of paper, and transfer the design to the stencil paper by tracing it or by using carbon paper. Place a cutting board or piece of thick card under the stencil paper, then, with a sharp pointed craft knife, cut around the shapes that will be printed. Work slowly and carefully to ensure an absolutely clean-cut edge. Make sure the template has a generous border all the way around to prevent paint running onto the fabric by mistake. Plastic sheet or thick acetate sheet is a very good alternative to stencil paper and has the advantage of being see-through. Sticky-backed plastic can be used several times.

Lift out the cutaway shape with the point of your knife, cutting any small areas which fail to dislodge. Do not leave any torn or jagged edges. The template should last for many applications, but when it begins to wear, make another by painting through onto another piece of stencil paper.

Stencilling fabric

Begin by spreading out your fabric on a smooth, flat, paper-covered work surface. Secure it with masking tape, and secure the stencil to the fabric with masking tape or spray mount glue.

Then prepare the paints. The consistency should be that of thick custard. If you use fabric paints, check beforehand that the colours don't bleed under the stencil. If they do, add a thickener so they can be used for stencilling.

Using a brush

Dip the stencil brush into the paint and then dab it on a paper towel to remove any excess. The brush should be almost dry. Apply the paint lightly to the fabric by dabbing it through the cut-out spaces of the stencil. Work slowly and deliberately from the outer edge to the inside of each shape. Make sure your stencil does not move, otherwise you will blur the image. Build up more colour in some places by going over the same area several times. Use darker and lighter shades of the same colour to form shadows and highlights.

When the paint is dry, remove the tape, and

carefully lift the stencil. Check the underside of the stencil for damp colour and remove with a paper towel if any is present. Reposition the stencil and proceed as before, applying the paint in stipples.

In the case of an all-over repeat in which the shapes of a unit touch each other, it is best to stencil every other unit first and later fill in the blanks. This avoids the problem of placing the border of the stencil in damp colour. Mark out the fabric carefully, using a water-soluble pen, so that the stencil can be placed accurately.

Using a sponge

Dampen the sponge slightly. Pour a small amount of paint into a saucer, press a corner of the sponge into it, then dab off the paint on a paper towel until the sponge is nearly dry. Lightly dab the sponge onto the cut-out areas.

Using a stencil crayon

Rub some colour from a stick onto an uncut piece of the stencil. Work the colour into the bristles of a brush in a circular motion. Use the brush to work the colour over the cut-out shape, moving in a circular motion from the outside towards the centre. Shading is easier with a crayon than with paint, but allow plenty of drying time.

Using a blow spray/diffuser or spray can

Spraying dye onto fabric can give a wonderful, stippled texture. It is fun and simple to do. But it can be messy, so wear an overall and protect the areas you do not want sprayed with newspaper. Work outside or in a well-ventilated room.

Dip one end of a diffuser into a narrow container of dye. Make sure the dye comes at least halfway up the diffuser. Blow gently from the diaphragm. It will take a bit of time to master the technique without creating unwanted blobs. Apply a thin

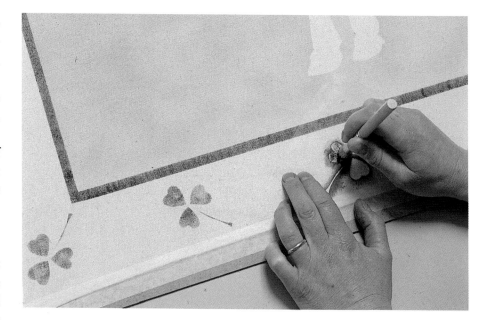

▲ Using a stencil brush, apply paint by dabbing it through the cut-out spaces of the stencil.

layer of dye and allow it to dry, then repeat. Do not spray too thickly or the dye will run.

When you have completed your stencilling, there may be a few small gaps between units or an uneven area. Touch these up with direct application of colour and a small brush. Allow the fabric to dry and then fix or finish as required. Leave the stencilled fabric for two weeks before washing.

Cleaning stencils and brushes

Clean card stencils with a paper towel or rag dipped in water for water-based paints and white spirit for solvent-based sprays. Rinse plastic stencils under the tap or wipe with white spirit. Store stencils flat, separated with sheets of newspaper. Wash stencil brushes with the appropriate cleaner.

Before embarking on a project you should spend time mixing and experimenting with paints on the fabric you are actually going to use. The fabric paint often dries lighter than you expect so wait to see how your test strips of fabric turn out.

Stencilled floor cloth

Floor cloths used to be very popular in Europe and America during the 18th century. They were considered to be the poor man's alternative to rugs and carpets until linoleum and wall-to-wall carpets became popular. But now floor cloths can be appreciated in their own right. They look very attractive when placed over a wooden floor or tiles.

You will need:

- Scissors
- Heavyweight cotton duck or canvas
- Frame or board
- 2 large paintbrushes
- Emulsion paint
- PVA adhesive
- Sandpaper
- Pencil and paper
- Tracing paper
- Stencil acetate or card
- Cutting board
- Masking tape
- Stencil knife
- Acrylic paints
- Clean palette or saucers
- Sponge
- Stencilling brushes
- Oil-based stencil crayon
- Spray mount glue
- Matt varnish
- Canvas or carpet felt for backing

► After spraying on the background colour, gently peel away the cow template.

YOU CAN PAINT OR STENCIL ANY DESIGN ON the canvas and then varnish it so that it can withstand wear and tear.

When stencilling a floor cloth, the major problem will be to find enough space to stretch it and work on it. The best thing to do is to stretch the canvas over a home-made wooden frame or staple it to a large piece of plywood. You will also need good ventilation, as you will be using primer, paints and varnish which all give off fumes.

1 Cut the canvas to the required size, remembering to allow enough material so that you have a selvedge of 7.5cm (3in) around the edge. This should be left unprimed. Stretch the canvas on a frame or board.

2 Prime the surface of the canvas with a mixture of 4 parts emulsion paint to 1 part PVA adhesive to give the surface greater flexibility. Tint this to the shade required for the background. Stipple the paint well into the weave of the canvas to build up a flat, smooth surface.

3 When the first coat is dry, sand it lightly and apply a second. Allow it to dry thoroughly and sand it again. Apply at least three layers of paint, sanding each layer to make the surface of the floor cloth smooth. It is now ready for stencilling.

4 Draw out the design of the cow stencil on paper, and then trace it onto the stencil acetate/card as described

above. Fix the stencil to the cutting board with masking tape. Cut out the areas you want to be black in the cow design. Make a template of the cow out of paper.

5 Prepare your paints in separate saucers. Remember to blend enough of each colour so that you do not run out when you are halfway through your stencilling.

6 Use a pencil and masking tape to mark the border line. Stencil with a sponge between the masking tape lengths. Allow to dry, then remove the masking tape to reveal the border. Stencil a border of clover leaves with a stencil brush. Offsetting the stencil very slightly, stencil with paint around the edges to create an offset outline like a shadow.

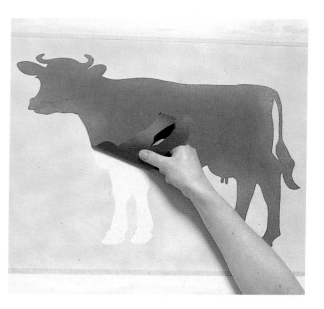

► Using a sponge, dab the paints for the cow's body through the stencil onto the canvas.

7 Next take the template of the cow. Spray glue it and position it on the fabric. Cover with paper the areas you don't want sprayed. Spray the colour and let it dry. Remove the template and fix the cow stencil into position with spray mount glue or masking tape. Use a sponge to apply the paints to the canvas through the stencil. Use separate stencils for the horns, hooves and udder.

8 When the stencilling is complete and the paints are dry, seal the surface with several coats of PVA diluted with water. Allow the PVA to dry thoroughly between each coat. Finally apply a coat of matt varnish to tone down the glossy finish of the PVA.

▼ Using a separate stencil, apply the paint for the hooves with a stencil crayon.

9 When this is dry, turn the floor cloth over. Sand the back lightly to remove the bobbles of paint that will have come through from the first application of paint.

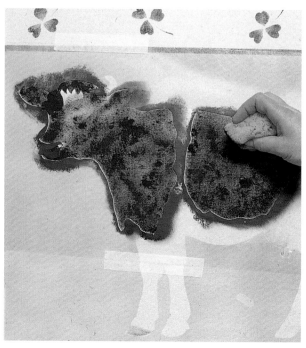

10 Using PVA, glue down the edges of the floor cloth making a neat corner. This may need weighting down at the corners while it dries.

11 When the floor cloth is dry, sew or glue a backing onto it. For this you can use either another layer of canvas or carpet felt. Cut it to fit neatly so that the floor cloth has no ridges on the back.

12 Whenever the surface of the floor cloth becomes worn through wear and tear, apply more layers of varnish. Never fold the floor cloth as the paint might crack. Always pick it up by rolling it loosely.

M a r b l i n g

You will need:

- Size (a mixture of water and gelatine)
- Marbling tank (a large shallow tray about 7.5cm (3in) deep)
- Oil paints or water-based fabric paints
- White spirit
- Paintbrushes
- Ox gall (or washing-up liquid)
- Pipettes, eye-droppers or fine brushes
- Cocktail sticks, combs, or knitting needles
- Pieces of fabric smaller than the marbling tray (cotton, silk or wool)
- Bowl of water
- 5ml (1tsp) vinegar
- Newspaper
- Iron
- Mild detergent
- 2 small pieces of dowelling rod (optional)

MARBLING ON PAPER IS AN ANCIENT JAPANESE art. Its attractive swirls of colour and pattern became very popular in Europe and marbling was used particularly by bookbinders for the inside of their books. However, marbling can be used just as easily on fabric. The basic principle is the same. Oily paints are floated over the surface of water. By thickening the water with size, you have better control over the patterns. If you gently lay a piece of paper or fabric on the surface and then lift it up, the paint pattern will be transferred to it.

Experiment at first with marbling on paper, mainly because it is cheaper than fabric. Once you have gained some confidence in controlling the pattern, try marbling on small pieces of fabric.

PREPARING THE MARBLING SIZE

The consistency of the size is crucial to the success of the marbling. You will need to thicken the water until it is like wallpaper paste. This makes it easier

▶ Tap a paintbrush laden with paint against a stick to spatter paint over the surface of the size.

to spread the colours and draw all kinds of patterns in the inks. Usually carragheen moss (which is a seaweed) is used to thicken the water, but you can use wallpaper paste, gelatine or a powdered marbling ground (available from art suppliers) which are easy to mix. Oil colour can produce effective results when floated *just* on water, but it is difficult to control and spread into patterns. You can control the patterns better when you use a size.

Wallpaper-paste size Pour 1 litre (32fl oz) cold water into a bowl and gradually sprinkle in the paste powder until the mixture looks like runny jelly. Stir well so that lumps are prevented from forming. When it is mixed, leave the size to thicken slightly. Dilute it until it is the consistency of thin cream. Pour it into your dish to a depth of about 7.5cm (3in) and leave to stand for about 30 minutes before using.

Carragheen moss size This is the best method of all and the patterns are more controllable. Pour 1 litre (32fl oz) cold water into a saucepan. Add 30g (1oz) dried carragheen moss with 1 tablespoon borax (this prevents the carragheen moss from separating). Bring slowly to the boil, stirring well until the mixture thickens. Simmer for 5 minutes. Remove from heat and add another litre (32fl oz) cold water. Leave to stand overnight. Do not allow the size to get too cold or else it will get lumpy; nor too hot as the colours will become uncontrollable. The size will keep for two or three days but you can freeze it if you want to use it at a later date. Always have a little extra size at hand so that you can top up your marbling base. Before you use it, strain the size through a layer of muslin into a bowl and carefully add some more water — between 1–3 litres (1½–4¾pt) depending on the result

wanted. The size should be as thin as possible as long as the paints do not sink. If the paints do not spread on the surface then the size is probably too thick. The process of making a carragheen moss base requires great care but the results are worth it.

BASIC TECHNIQUE

Cover the work surface with newspaper. Prepare the marbling size (see above), and pour it into the container that you are going to marble in.

Squeeze about 2cm (¾in) of the oil paint from the tube and dilute with white spirit, mixing it well until it is like thin cream. Add a few drops of ox gall (or try a little washing-up liquid) to each colour and mix well into the paints. Using a pipette or fine brush, gently apply drops of colour onto the surface of the size. Alternatively, using a household paintbrush, carefully flick or spatter the colour onto the size until almost the entire surface has been covered with paint. Experiment with three or four colours and work from dark to light and vice versa. Each new colour will disperse the others over the surface of the size. (White is very useful and gives a separation to the colours but if you want a dark and rich effect, then don't use it.) Draw a comb or knitting needle gently through the colours and you will see a lovely swirly pattern emerge.

When the design looks satisfactory, lift the fabric holding two sides, and *carefully* lower it onto the marbling surface. Avoid trapping air bubbles beneath the fabric. If it is a large piece of fabric, you may need the help of an extra pair of hands. Fabric is trickier than paper. Leave for a few seconds for the fabric to pick up the oil paints, and lift it off, without dragging it across the surface. You will find the pattern has cleanly transferred onto the fabric.

◀ Draw a knitting needle gently through the spattered size to create a lovely feathery pattern.

If you used oil-based paints, immerse the fabric in a bowl containing 2.5 litres (4pt) water and 5ml (1tsp) vinegar to remove the moss or wallpaper paste solution and excess paint. Lay the fabric on newspaper, right side up, and leave to dry for a few hours. If you used water-based paints, let the marbled fabric dry naturally: don't wash off the excess size. Iron the fabric, and then wash in detergent and warm water and hang up to dry. If you used fabric paints, iron-fix them for at least five minutes before you wash the fabric. Oil paints do not need fixing.

Any paint left on the base tray can be used to create a lighter copy of the design on another piece of fabric. Otherwise, skim off any remaining ink with strips of newspaper, and add more paint for your next print. You can use as many colours as you like but when you drag the colour in lines or swirls do it very gently. If you stir it up too much it can look like a muddy mess.

Making patterns

Every time you marble, the pattern will be different. The kind of tool you use will determine the type of pattern created. Thin sticks or a knitting needle can be used to pull the paint into swirling patterns, while an old comb with a few teeth missing or a homemade comb will give a more streaked effect. Pull the colours until you are pleased with the design. Make sure the base is absolutely clean when you want to introduce different colours.

Hints

● If you use water-based paints you will have to prepare your fabric with a mordant so that the dye colour soaks into the fabric. This is usually alum (which can be bought at chemists). Dissolve 4 heaped teaspoons of alum in 1 litre (32fl oz) hot water. Submerge the silk in this mixture for five minutes, then hang up to dry. Iron gently with a cool iron. The fixative will keep in a screw-top jar until needed.

● If the colour disperses too quickly over the surface of the size, the size is not thick enough. Mix up extra ground so you can add a few drops of it if necessary to hold the colour correctly.

● When you wish to marble large pieces of fabric, lay four battens on the table with a double thickness of polythene on them, dipping in the centre. Make sure the corners are supported and that the solution will not pour out. Fill with whichever medium you are going to use. It is much easier if there are two people to handle the fabric, one at each end. Another way is to pin the two sides of the fabric to a piece of dowelling, each the same length as the fabric. Hold one side in each hand, and lay the fabric down on the size.

▲ To make a print, hold two sides of a piece of fabric, and carefully lower it onto the marbling surface. Leave in place for a few seconds before lifting it off.

Marbled photograph frame

Try making an attractive fabric-covered photograph frame from your marbled silk or satin. You could then go on to create a series of toning marbled frames in which to display your favourite photographs. Even if you marble with the same colours each time, the pattern will always be different.

You will need:

- Piece of marbled silk or satin, 22.5cm × 17.5cm (9in × 7in)
- Scissors
- Piece of plain mount card, 20cm × 15cm (8in × 6in)
- Wadding, 21cm × 16.5cm (8½in × 6½in)
- PVA glue
- Cutting board
- Sharp craft knife
- Piece of gold or silver mount card, 20cm × 15cm (8in × 6in) for backing
- Acetate film
- 2 small pieces of dowelling rod

▶ Stretch the marbled silk over the wadding and secure the edges to the back of the card frame with glue.

1 Marble a piece of silk or satin a little larger than the measurements above. Once it is dry choose the best part and cut to size.

2 Cut a window in the plain mount card, leaving a border of 3cm (1¼in) on three sides and 3.5cm (1⅜in) for the bottom of the frame.

3 Take the wadding and stretch it around the mount. Fold over the edges and glue to the back of the card.

4 When the glue has dried and the wadding is taut, use a pair of sharp scissors to pierce a hole in the centre of the wadding. Make cuts from the centre to each inner corner of the window.

5 Trim the wadding and fold over the inner edges, gluing them on the back.

6 Stretch your piece of silk over the wadding, and secure the edges with glue to the back of the card. Pierce through the centre of the silk and make similar cuts as you did with the wadding. Trim the silk, turn over the edges and glue to the back of the card. This can be a bit fiddly so be patient.

7 Once the silk is secure and the glue is dry, you can now attach the padded front of the frame to the backing card. Apply glue to the edges of the wrong side of the card (about

12mm (½in) along three edges, leaving the top edge unglued). Stick the backing card to the padded front so that the gold or silver colouring is visible from the back.

8 Score the support card, glue the top of it and stick it to the centre of the back of the frame. (The bottom of the support piece should be in line with the bottom of the frame when it lies flat.)

9 Once the glue has dried, cut a piece of acetate film slightly smaller than the size of the frame and insert it between the front and back of the frame. Slide in a picture or photograph and stand the frame on your desk or mantelpiece.

Techniques of Resist Dyeing

Unlike surface painting, where paint or dye is applied to the surface of fabric, resist dyeing involves *dye penetrating* the fabric. To control the spread of the dye, you must create a barrier or *resist*, which in this section is either starch, gutta or wax. Resist dyeing, therefore, involves a series of stages in which you apply the resist onto areas of the fabric you do *not* want dye to encroach upon. The easiest way to understand how this works is to have a go. So read on . . .

Resist dyeing

IN THIS SECTION OF THE BOOK WE WILL BE USING different kinds of dyes, silk paints, reactive and cold water dyes. These are formulated to run and spread through the fibres of fabrics so you can create effects which are not possible with emulsion-based paints, which are used for surface painting.

The best fabrics for resist dyeing are ones with natural fibres in them. Natural fibres are divided into cellulose (plant fibres) or protein (animal fibres). Cellulose fibres include cotton, linen and viscose rayon. Protein fibres include silk and wool. All natural fibres are good for tie-dyeing and batik. But dyes bond with fibres in different ways. Some dyes will produce more vivid colours with cellulose fibres than they will with protein fibres, and vice versa. Synthetic fibres do not dye well.

DYES

The dyes I have used in this section are water-soluble. They penetrate the fibres of fabrics and colour them.

Silk dyes These are ideal for gutta and wax resist techniques. They have a transparent, shimmering quality to them when they are applied to silk. Start at first with three colours – clear yellow, cyan blue and fuchsia (magenta). From these three you can mix most of the colours you will want. If you add black, then you can make any shade you need.

Cotton dyes The dyes that I usually use on cotton are cold water fibre-reactive dyes. *Reactive dyes* form a stable, direct chemical link with natural fibres that can be found in cotton and linen. They can also be used on silk. The dyes are exceptionally clear and have excellent fastness to light and washing. They are available from craft shops. The colour possibilities obtainable with the cold water reactive dyes are almost unlimited. However,

remember that after a dyebath has been prepared and used once, it is considered spent and shouldn't be used again.

Dyeing is a chemical process so you should treat the chemicals *carefully* and store them with care. Here are some points to remember:

- Protect the area where the dyeing is to take place with newspaper or polythene sheeting. Take care not to splash the dye as it is liable to stain easily.
- Do not use the area for any other activity at the same time. Dyes are poisonous and should not be eaten or inhaled. If possible, wear a dust mask when you mix the dyes.
- Wear an overall and rubber gloves when you are mixing the dyes and dyeing the fabric.
- Make sure any bowls and brushes you need for dyeing are kept clean.

PREPARING FABRIC

Fabric has to be prepared before you can resist-dye. It is often treated with a stiffening agent called size which must be removed. Wash the fabric in hot, soapy water, then rinse, dry and iron it. Several washes may be needed.

In certain resist techniques, for example batik, you need to rinse the fabric before dyeing. Fabrics are usually dyed wet so that the dye can impregnate the fibre more easily and evenly.

After dyeing, wash all utensils, brushes, washing line and pegs thoroughly in hot water and detergent before storing.

When you have dyed any fabric, make a note of exactly what you have done and what recipe you have used. Keep a square of fabric next to the recipe and instructions, for reference.

Dyeing can be complicated but the dyes mentioned in this book are easy to use as long as you read and follow the manufacturer's instructions.

Starch resist

STARCH OR PASTE RESIST IS A TRADITIONAL method of resist dyeing which is used in many parts of the world, especially Nigeria and Japan. It is cheap, quick and easy to do. Starch paste, which can be made from wheat flour, soya flour, rice flour, ground rice and laundry starch, is painted onto fabric to act as a resist to dyes and paints.

The advantage of this method is that you do not need much equipment. Even children enjoy doing it but they have to learn to be patient as the starch takes a long time to dry. Use starch resist when you wish to obtain the unique characteristic crackle it produces. This is often best seen when the design is kept to the simplest shapes. The effects are unlike anything that you can get with batik (wax resist). The chief drawback of starch resist is that all pastes are water soluble, so if you dip the pasted pieces of fabric in dye, the paste will quickly become soggy and the dye will reach the underside of the printed cotton, producing a lighter colour. It is more usual to brush or sponge the dye over the pasted surface.

▼ Apply starch paste with a brush or plastic bottle with a nozzle to get clear, graceful lines.

MAKING STARCH PASTE

The simplest recipe for starch paste is to mix white flour to a paste with water, but this *mixed paste recipe* will produce a different effect:

Mix 1 tablespoon each of rice flour and white flour, and ½ tablespoon powdered laundry starch in cold water and stir until the lumps have gone. Add the mixture to ½ litre (15fl oz) water and heat in the top of a double boiler for 10 minutes. Stir frequently. The mixture should be semi-translucent and the consistency of thin mashed potatoes.

Apply the paste while hot. Either use a brush or spoon some paste into a plastic bottle with a nozzle and gently squeeze the paste onto the fabric. Squeeze with an even pressure to get clear, graceful lines.

Allow the paste to dry thoroughly. This will take at least 24 hours. The paste will shrink and crack as it dries. Then apply fabric paint or thickened dye (not liquid dye) over the surface of the fabric with a sponge or dab colour on with a brush. The paint will seep through the cracks in the paste onto the fabric.

If you stretch the fabric on a frame and then apply the paste, the *paste* will crack as it dries. However, if you lay the fabric unstretched on newspaper and apply paste on top, the *fabric* will crumple as the paste dries. Pull the fabric to straighten it out and cracks will occur. If you want more cracks gently crumple the fabric in your hand.

When the fabric is dry, rub off the paste. It should be crumbly. Scrape the rest off with a palette knife. Iron the fabric to set the paint, or heat-fix the colour in an oven at 150°C (300°F, Gas Mark 2) for 3–5 minutes. Wash the fabric in warm water to remove the final remains of the paste, then rinse and allow to dry.

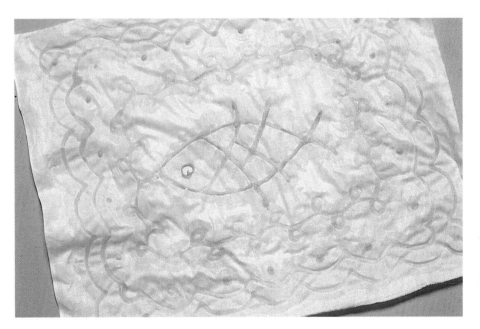

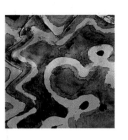

Starch paste table mats

Table mats are very useful and can brighten up a kitchen table. They are easy to make from hemmed rectangles of fabric. But here I have explained how to make an attractive variation – a padded table mat. The best material to use is white cotton cambric but you can try other thicknesses of fabric. An average size for a table mat is 30cm × 40cm (12in × 16in).

You will need:
(Makes one table mat)
- Piece of fabric, 36cm × 46cm (14in × 18in), for the backing
- Wadding, 30cm × 40cm (12in × 16in)
- Piece of starch-resisted fabric, 30cm × 40cm (12in × 16in) for the front of the mat
- Pins
- Sewing machine
- Needle and thread

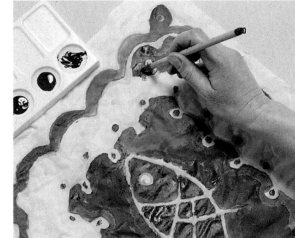

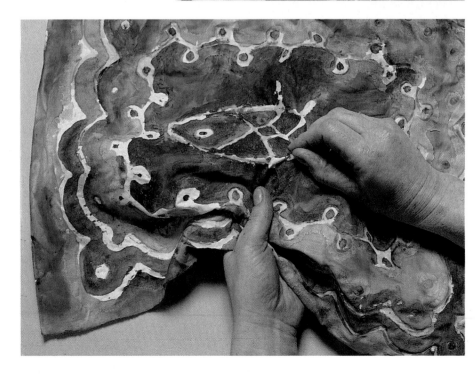

1 Starch resist the fabric following the instructions above. If you plan to make a set of table mats, choose a simple design that can be repeated. They will always vary slightly.

2 When the dyed fabric has been iron-fixed, lay the front piece of fabric right side down on the work surface. Place the wadding on top. Pin and tack into place. Quilt by machine stitching, if desired.

3 Place the backing fabric on the front fabric with right sides facing. Pin and tack into place. Machine around the edges, leaving a small gap so you can turn the mat inside out. Trim the seams and corners.

4 Turn the mat inside out and press. Slip-stitch to finish. Machine around the edges following your pattern. This helps to strengthen the mat.

▲ Apply fabric paint or thickened dye over the dried paste on the fabric.

◄ When the fabric is dry, rub off the crumbly paste with your fingers.

Gutta

GUTTA IS A THICK LIQUID LATEX WHICH, WHEN applied to fabric, acts as a resist. It is mainly used in combination with painting on silk. Silk paints applied freely to fabric can produce breathtakingly beautiful colours, subtle blends and patterns (see Freehand painting, page 30). But sometimes you don't want a colour to merge into another so a barrier or line can be drawn with the gutta to create clearly defined shapes on the silk. The silk paints are then applied carefully within the shapes and the colour is contained.

There are two types of gutta: water-soluble and spirit-based. Learn how to use the water-based one first as it is easier to remove at the end. As you become more confident, use the spirit-based gutta for more reliable and professional results. If the water-soluble gutta does not penetrate the fabric it is too thick. Thin it out with a little water. If the spirit-based gutta is too thick, use the manufacturer's own diluent. After the dyes have been fixed, remove the water-based gutta by washing the fabric in a mild detergent and water. Remove spirit-based gutta by squeezing the silk in white spirit after steam fixing.

You can apply the gutta with a sponge or brush but, for drawing, use a plastic bottle (pipette) with a nozzle. Cut the tip off the nozzle and squeeze lines and dots of resist onto silk. A special pen nib can be attached for very fine detail.

HINT: It is easier to control the flow of gutta if the resist applicator is at least three-quarters full.

BASIC METHOD
Any lightweight silk can be used with this technique. So can a lightweight cotton but it is more difficult to see the clear gutta on this so try a silver or black gutta. Before you begin, wash the silk and stretch the fabric on a frame. Make sure it is smooth and taut, with no dips or ridges.

Fill a pipette with gutta then, holding the pipette like a pen, draw with it, squeezing the gutta out gently. When you have finished the gutta outline, hold the fabric to the light to see if there are any gaps in your lines. If so fill them in with more gutta.

Allow the gutta to dry out thoroughly – for about 24 hours – before applying any paint. Using a fine watercolour brush or a cotton bud, apply the paint carefully as it is easy to flood paint over the gutta barrier into the next space.

Work steadily and fairly fast in order to avoid any streaking of the paint. For large areas use a sponge brush as you can cover the ground more quickly. Allow the paint to dry before you remove the fabric from the frame. Fix the colour by ironing, wash the gutta out in cold water and dry.

HINT: Remove smudged gutta with a cotton bud dipped in water, white spirit or a manufacturer's solvent.

▼ When the gutta is dry, carefully apply the paint with a fine watercolour brush.

Gutta silk scarf *(pictured on page 69)*

Once you feel confident with the gutta technique, try making this silk scarf. You could copy my design for a fruity scarf, or you could follow the techniques below, substituting your own design and colour scheme.

You will need:
- Pencil and paper
- Black pen
- Tracing paper
- Soft pencil/ disappearing fabric-marking pen
- 1m (40in) square of silk (habotai, medium or heavyweight) *or a* ready-handrolled scarf
- Frame
- Masking tape or silk pins
- Plastic bottle with nib
- Gutta
- Silk dyes
- Pointed watercolour brushes, sponge brushes, cotton buds, cotton wool pads
- Palette or saucers
- Diluent
- Salt crystals and alcohol, optional

▲ Apply the dyes with a paintbrush, allowing the colours to blend.

▶ To colour the background, sponge the area with water, then apply the dyes while the silk is still damp.

1 Draw out the design on paper. Go around the outline in black pen and trace the image onto the silk with a soft pencil or a special disappearing fabric-marking pen.

2 Stretch the silk onto the frame. You can use masking tape or fine silk pins to secure the silk to the wood. Make sure the silk is taut and has no ripples in it.

3 Using the plastic bottle with nib, draw along the lines with the gutta. Leave for 24 hours to dry thoroughly.

4 Apply the colours with a paintbrush. Start with the fruit around the border. Allow the colours to blend to create the textures of the apples and pears. If you want an even distribution of colour for the background, sponge the areas of the silk with a little water or a special liquid called diluent. Paint on the dyes while the silk is damp. If you want texture, add drops of alcohol or water. Also sprinkle salt onto the damp silk if you want a mottled, swirly effect (see Freehand painting, page 30).

5 You can over-dye, but apply the purest and lightest hue to the surface and progress to the deepest and darkest. If you want to paint details, like the spots on the fruit or leaves, dilute the gutta (with water if it is water-based) and paint it onto the selected areas. Allow to dry properly. Use a small brush to apply the fine lines and dots, and you will find that the dye will hardly run.

6 Allow the dyes to dry naturally. Iron the silk to fix the colours. Wash the scarf in mild detergent and lukewarm water to remove the water-based gutta. Damp-dry and iron again.

7 If making your own scarf, handroll the edges of the scarf, and slip-stitch in place.

B a t i k

THIS IS MY FAVOURITE TECHNIQUE, SO I HAVE found it hard to limit it to only a few pages. Batik is effective, easy to do and can be used for decorating fabric for clothing, home furnishings and for creating pictures. However, because the dyes penetrate the fabric, making the dye and fabric as one, it has a transparent and unique quality which can be shown to its best advantage when light is shone from behind.

If you understand the principle that wax and water don't mix, then you will be halfway to understanding how batik works. Batik is a resist method of dyeing and decorating fabric. Molten wax is used to prevent the dyes from penetrating the fibres of the fabric. Different tools can be used to apply the wax, each adding its own character to the quality of line and texture. The method originated in the Middle East, India and the Far East, but it is in Java, Indonesia, where the most accomplished batiks can be seen. Nowadays batik is used all over the world for clothing, table linen, decorating fabric and for creating pictures. The word 'batik' comes from the Javanese word *ambatik*, derived from *tik* which means to mark with a point, dot or drop.

WHAT YOU NEED

Batik wax Ready-mixed batik wax is available from craft suppliers but try out other waxes, or mix your own (for example, 1 part paraffin wax, 1 part beeswax and 1 part microcrystalline wax) to achieve different effects.

Wax pot This can either be a thermostatically-controlled wax pot; an electric frying pan that has a built-in temperature control; or you can use a double boiler with a water compartment and an electric ring.

Smooth fabrics Natural fine fabrics like fine cotton (lawn, cambric) and silk are most suitable.

Frame The fabric should be stretched on a frame to make a taut, flat surface and held with staples or fine drawing pins. You can use wooden batik frames, canvas stretchers or embroidery rings.

Cantings (pronounced tjanting) The canting is a Javanese tool used for applying the wax. It consists of a small copper container or reservoir with a short wooden handle and a thin spout (or spouts). The spout is used for drawing wax lines onto the material. There are several kinds of canting available.

Brushes These are for applying the wax. The preferred types are bristle or natural hair, for example sable, but not synthetic brushes as they are susceptible to melting in hot wax. A Chinese brush is ideal as it can hold a lot of wax and yet produce a fine line with its point.

Newspapers and **paper towels** Essential for blotting, catching drips and protecting table surfaces.

Cold water dyes Do not use hot water dyes as the heat will melt the wax. Be certain that the dye has an affinity for the fabric being used. Cold water fibre-reactive dyes are suitable both for dipping and for painting on. Choose the basic colours – lemon-yellow, scarlet, cerise, turquoise and a navy blue or black. Most other colours can be mixed from these.

Watercolour brushes, sponge brushes, etc, for applying the dye.

Empty jars for the mixed dyes.

Pencil Use a soft lead, such as a 2B or 4B.

Plastic bucket or **plastic container** This should be large enough for the fabric to be totally immersed if you are dip-dyeing.

Rubber gloves Essential when using dyes.

Iron

Drying rack or **clothes line**

Drawing pins or **silk pins**

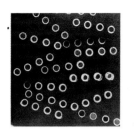

TECHNIQUE OF BATIK

First wash the fabric and rinse it to remove the size. After drying and ironing your fabric, stretch it taut over a frame and don't allow it to touch the paper below. Do not worry what you are going to draw at first – just experiment.

HEATING THE WAX

Take care not to overheat the wax. It needs to be kept at a constant temperature (somewhere between 49°C (120°F) and 60°C (140°F). If the temperature goes below 49°C (120°F) the wax will not flow that easily and will be less likely to penetrate the fabric satisfactorily. If the wax becomes too hot, it will start smoking, which is both smelly and dangerous. Never leave the hot wax unattended.

USING A BRUSH

The brush is an excellent tool for applying wax. The technique is quite simple and not unlike painting. You can use fine brushes for detail

▼ Practise making different marks on the fabric with the brush and melted wax.

drawing or filling small spaces, and large brushes for covering large areas. If you have to wax a background, outline all areas to be waxed with a small brush then fill them in with a large one.

Dip the brush into the molten wax, wipe any drips away with a paper towel and draw on the fabric. When hot wax touches the fabric it has a tendency to spread as well as penetrate so keep the brush moving or a sizeable blob or dot will develop. You will find that the wax cools quickly while you are working so dip the brush into the wax frequently to ensure the wax is hot enough to penetrate the fabric. Make different marks with the brush and wax. Use the side of the brush for outlines and the width for broad line work.

A fine, spattered effect can be obtained by tapping your wax-filled bristle against a ruler or brush handle. Protect areas that do not require spattering with a stencil or paper. Also cover your work surface with a sheet of plastic or newspaper.

You can etch lines in the waxed fabric with a pointed metal tool. Do the same on the reverse side, following the same lines, but take care not to pierce the fabric. The process is known as *sgraffito*.

You will find that the wax dries on impact, so once you have finished the first stage of waxing, you can paint a colour or dye over the waxed areas and see your results immediately. The waxed fabric stays white while the uncovered parts turn the colour of your dye. If you want to retain some of the first colour, wax those areas and apply a second dye and so on. Many subtle shades of colour can be built up in this way.

Batik is often known by its unique characteristic crackle or marble effect. This is caused by the wax cracking or breaking down, allowing the colour or dye to seep through the cracks. Cover the entire piece, the background or just a section with large strokes of wax. Work quickly, returning the brush frequently to the wax pot to keep the wax hot and flowing. Check the back of your work to see whether the wax has penetrated and sealed the fibres so that they will resist the dye. When the wax has cooled (this only takes a few seconds) remove the fabric from the frame and crush the waxed areas firmly between your hands with a gentle, even pressure. Don't overdo it. Too much crackle will let the dye flood under the wax layer.

Paint on a dark dye or dip the fabric into a bowl of dye, and check the effect on the crackled areas.

HINTS: Do not leave a brush in melted wax too long or it may become misshapen and might start losing its bristles. Your brush will gradually harden once exposed to the air. To soften it again, simply re-dip your brush into the wax.

The fabric must be dry before you apply the wax. If it is not you will find that the wax will sit on the surface and will not penetrate the fibres. The dye will then creep under the wax and spoil your design.

USING SPONGE OR PAPER

For a more textured effect, try using latex foam or paper. Using a pair of scissors cut shapes out of the foam and then dip the foam into the wax. Press the waxed foam onto the fabric. In most places the wax print will be bold with soft, textured edges. Crumpled-up paper can also be very effective, as well as the textured surface of a paper towel. Dip the rolled-up paper towel into the wax, being careful not to overload it. Wipe off the excess, and gently print the wax onto the fabric. With practice you should be able to capture the textured quality of the paper towel.

USING A STAMP

In Java most batiks are stamp-printed today. Intricate designs are made from copper stripping and are attached to a frame forming a stamp or cap. The cap is pressed into a wax-soaked pad before being printed onto the fabric. This process is repeated until the whole fabric has been waxed. The fabric is then reversed and matching stamps

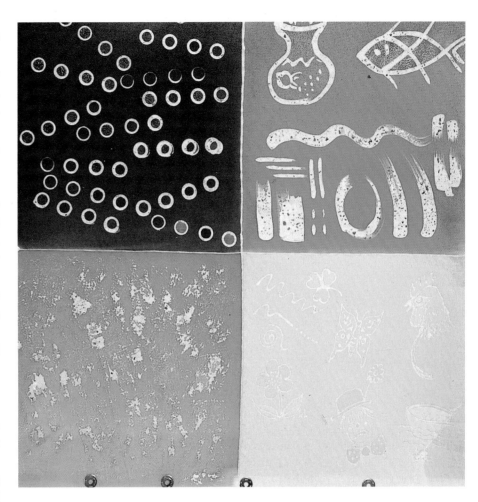

are applied to ensure a complete resist.

You can make your own stamp by: pushing nails into cork; bending wire into a decorative shape, and leaving a handle to hold it by; or using ready-made stamps, for example a potato masher.

Dip the stamp into the hot wax for a minute to warm up. Then lift it out and shake gently to remove any excess. Press it onto the stretched fabric. For a better defined print do a quick print of the stamp onto some paper to remove excess wax and then press it firmly onto the fabric. Refuel and repeat the pattern.

USING A CANTING

A canting is usually used for wax drawing or *tulis* work (*tulis* is a Javanese word meaning hand-

▲ Create different batik effects by applying wax with a homemade stamp (top left), a brush (top right), a rolled-up paper towel (bottom left) or a canting (bottom right).

drawing the wax resist). Experiment with it. You will find that you will only need a little practice to learn how to handle a canting. It can be a versatile and exciting tool to use. The canting is held between the forefinger and the thumb with the handle held inside the palm of the hand. To fill it, dip it into molten wax, holding it down long enough for the copper bowl to be heated through so that the wax does not congeal too quickly while you are working. Do not overfill the canting bowl or the wax will spill over onto the material.

Raise the canting above the wax and wipe the spout with a piece of paper towel to prevent any wax dropping onto the material. Hold the paper towel under the spout when you transfer the canting to the material, and keep it close at hand during the waxing process for catching drips. If wax does drip onto the fabric by mistake, don't worry! Just incorporate the mistake into the final design.

As you draw the canting smoothly towards you across the fabric a waxed line will be drawn. The wax will sink into the fabric, spreading slightly and becoming transparent. If the wax is too hot it will flow more quickly along the spout and the line will become thicker. Keep the canting moving. If you stop, blobs of wax will occur along your line. When making dots, work rhythmically.

If the wax is too cool, it will appear opaque on the fabric. It is important that the wax penetrates completely or it will not resist the dye and blurred lines will result when the dye is applied.

When the wax in the reservoir of the canting begins to cool, dip the canting back in the wax pot for a few seconds to reheat the wax.

Should any impurities, such as specks of dust or bits of thread, slow up the flow of wax, clear the spout with a very fine wire. Gently push the wire up the spout. If the wax flows too quickly then you can put a piece of cotton wool inside the reservoir to slow it down.

It is not necessary to clean the canting after use. Simply let the wax harden and the next time you use it, hold it downwards in the melted wax until the remains of the wax melt.

Designs made with a canting are usually distinguishable. You can make spirals and zigzag lines as well as dots and tear-drop shapes across your fabric. Alternatively, you could just make a series of curlicues or squiggly lines.

HINTS: Remember to remove your brushes and canting from the wax pot before turning the heat off. They can be damaged if you pull them out once the wax has hardened. Re-melt the wax to release them safely.

Always try to rest the canting on a rag or waxed paper, or prop it up so the copper reservoir is not touching anything when you are not using it. If you let it cool on something hard, the canting may stick to it and the little spout can get broken when it is being unstuck.

DYEING

There are two ways to dye batiked fabric. The more common method is by submersion or *dipping* in a dye solution. (For a fuller description, see Batiked cushion, page 75.) The second method is by *applying the dye directly*. A sponge or brush is generally used for applying dyes in this way.

You can apply the wax in a similar way as you apply gutta resist. You can outline shapes with a continuous line of wax, similar to the effect created by gutta resist. Apply the dye carefully with a brush, and you will find that the dye will stay within the shape. The general effect at the end is that of a leaded window except that the lines are light rather than dark. Iron the finished piece between absorbent paper and dry-clean it, if desired, to extract the last traces of wax.

You can also apply wax to certain areas to keep them white. Brush or sponge on dye at random, covering the surface of the fabric. When the colours are dry, wax those areas you want to protect and sponge over a darker dye.

Batiked cushion

Cushions are fun to design and if you make your own you can match it to the colours of your curtains or furniture. If you want to batik the cushion back to match the front, prepare this at the same time, to ensure the colours match.

You will need:
- Batik equipment, see page 71
- 2 pieces of white fabric measuring 45cm (18in) square
- Silk pins
- Cold water fibre-reactive dyes – yellow, turquoise and navy blue
- Needle and basting thread
- Sewing machine
- Zip fastener
- Pins
- Cushion pad

1 Wash and press the fabric to remove any dressing in it. Draw the design on the fabric with a soft pencil.

2 Stretch the fabric on the frame or stretcher by securing it with silk pins. Ensure the fabric is taut and that there are no dips or ridges in it.

3 Wax the areas that are to remain the lightest in the final piece. In this case the white areas are the petals of the waterlilies. Note that the waxed areas now appear darker than the unwaxed areas.

4 Make up a small quantity of yellow dye. Follow the instructions for the specific dye and be certain to wear rubber gloves. Paint the yellow dye onto the centre of the waterlilies. Allow to dry and wax the yellow stamens. Remove the fabric from the frame, rinse under cold water, and dye it in a pale turquoise colour.

5 Take the fabric out and rinse it well in running water. When the water runs clear, blot with paper towels and allow to dry. Notice that the unwaxed area has dyed turquoise-blue, while the waxed area has resisted the colour.

6 Stretch the fabric on the frame again. Apply wax to the areas that are to remain the blue colour, that is the water around the lily pads. Leave the lily pads unwaxed and leave gaps where you want the dye to penetrate. The waxed area looks darker than it really is. Hold the batik to the light occasionally to ascertain the true colour and judge the successive dyes.

7 Remove the fabric from the frame and dye it in the yellow colour. The lily pads and frog turn green while the water remains turquoise under the wax. Rinse and dry as before.

8 Stretch the fabric on the frame. Wax the lily pads and the frog. Leave unwaxed a gap for the outline, the frog markings and a few lily pads. Remove the fabric from the frame and dip it into a navy blue colour. The navy blue turns the green into a dark green. Now you have finished the waxing and dyeing process.

▶ Apply wax to the areas of the design that are to remain the lightest in colour in the final piece – the waterlily petals.

▲ Apply wax to the areas that are to remain blue in the final piece – the water around the lily pads.

9 *Once the fabric is dry, sandwich the finished batik between absorbent paper, preferably clean newsprint, and press with a hot iron. Replace the paper as it absorbs the wax.*

10 *There will still be a little wax in the fabric. To remove this residual wax, take it to the dry-cleaners. The fabric will be restored to its original state, only it will now have a design of a beautiful frog sitting on a waterlily! (To remove the residual wax, you can also squeeze the batik in white spirit for a few minutes and then wash it in a mild detergent. The smell of the white spirit dissipates in a few days.)*

FOR THE CUSHION BACK

Now you have a front to your cushion you can design your own picture for the back. Obviously it is advisable to think about what you want to do at the very beginning, so you can dip the fabric into the dye at the same time as the front piece. Then you would be certain that the colours of the

► Using a canting, apply fine line markings to the frog.

back matched the front. I chose to keep the design simple and so waxed a few streaks to make the back look as if it was water.

If you prefer, you could use a thicker fabric for the back. Press the front and back pieces of your frog cushion carefully.

SEWING UP THE CUSHION

1 *Place the two squares of fabric with right sides facing, and baste along one edge of the cushion cover. Allowing 12mm (½in) for the seam allowance, stitch 5cm (2in) at either end of the seam and press open.*

2 *Lay the zip fastener face-down on the wrong side of the fabric with teeth centred along the basted seam. Pin in place and then stitch. Remove the basting thread.*

3 *With right sides facing, stich the cushion cover together along the remaining three sides. Neaten the raw edges by zigzag stitching. Trim the corners.*

4 *Turn the cover right side out and press. Insert the cushion pad, poking it right into the corners.*

Useful addresses

Most fabrics, paints and dyes mentioned in this book can be bought in local artist's suppliers, fabric shops and DIY stores. Listed below are some retail outlets that you might find useful.

UK

Atlantis Paper Co Limited
2 St Andrews Way
London E3 3PA
Mail order. Silk dyes and silk-painting equipment

NES Arnold
Ludlow Hill Road
West Bridgeford
Nottingham NG2 6HD
Mail order. Fabric paints, pens and dyes, fabric, batik and silk-painting equipment, screen and block printing equipment

Berol
Old Meadow Road
King's Lynn
Norfolk PE30 4JR
Acrylic paint, lino-printing equipment and inks

Candlemakers' Supplies
28 Blythe Road
London W14 0HA
Shop and mail order. Silk paints, reactive and cold water dyes, wax, cantings, ready-made scarves, steaming service

Cornelissen and Son Ltd
105 Great Russell Street
London WC1B 3RY
Shop and mail order. Silk dyes and silk-painting equipment

Dryad Specialist Crafts Limited
PO Box 247
Leicester LE1 9QS
Mail order. Kits, silk-painting, fabric painting and printing equipment

Dylon International Limited
Worsley Bridge Road
Lower Sydenham
London SE26 5HD
Dyes

Noel Dyrenforth
11 Shepherds Hill
London N6
Mail order. Reactive dyes, cantings, workshops

Hays Chemical Limited
Bagnall House
55–57 Glengall Road
London SE15 6NQ
Silk dyes, reactive dyes, printing inks, indigo

Isaf Design Limited
The Barns
Cefn Isa
Cilcain
Mold
Clwyd CH7 5NT
Mail order. Silk dyes and kits

John Lewis
Oxford Street
London W1
Fabrics

Liquitex
Ampthill Road
Bedford MK42 9RS
Acrylic paints, fabric paints

MacCulloch & Wallis Limited
25–26 Dering Street
London W1R OBH
Fabrics – cottons and silks

The Painting on Silk Co
22 Wainwright Road
Altrincham
Cheshire WA14 4BW
Mail order. Silk-painting equipment, dyes, silk, gutta, steaming service

Pentel
Hunts Rise
South Marston Park
Swindon
Wiltshire SN3 4TW
Watercolour dyes, fabric pens and crayons

Philip & Tacey
North Way
Walworth Industrial Estate
Andover
Hampshire
Silk dyes, gutta, fabric crayons and pens, kits, printing equipment

Pongees Limited
184–186 Old Street
London EC1V 9FR
Silks

Russell & Chapple
33 Monmouth Street
London WC2
Fabric, canvas, stretchers

Village Crafts
Forest Row
West Sussex
Kits, silk paints, batik dyes

George Weil and Sons Limited
The Warehouse
Reading Arch Road
Redhill
Surrey RH1 1HG
and
18 Hanson Street (shop)
London W1P 7DB
Mail order. Fabrics – cotton, silk, fabric paints, batik equipment, cantings, reactive dyes, silk-painting dyes

Whaleys (Bradford) Limited
Harris Court
Great Horton
Bradford
West Yorkshire BD7 4EQ
Fabrics – cotton, silk, wool, linen

Index

ACKNOWLEDGEMENTS

I would like to thank the following for providing me with some of the materials used in this book: NES Arnold, Cade Crafts in Lewes, Candlemakers' Supplies, Noel Dyrenforth, George Weil & Sons, Isaf Design, Pentel, Philip & Tacey, Berol Limited, Liquitex, and Clarkes Stationer's in Haywards Heath, Sussex.

I would also like to thank Su Shephard, Noel Dyrenforth, Jon Bouchier and Sue Dowdall for all their help and support, and my family for being so patient and understanding. Finally I would like to thank Cumnor House School for their support and for allowing me to try out some of my ideas with the children.